D0898341

WITHDRAWN

Conversations
with Frederick
Manfred

Drawings by
Arnold John Dyson

Conversations with Frederick Manfred

Moderated by John R. Milton

with a Foreword by Wallace Stegner

The University of Utah Press   Salt Lake City

Contents

Books by Frederick Manfred, who wrote under the name of Feike Feikema from 1944 through 1951.

1944	The Golden Bowl
1945	Boy Almighty
1947	This Is the Year
1948	The Chokecherry Tree
1949	The Primitive
1950	The Brother
1951	The Giant
1954	Lord Grizzly
1956	Morning Red
1957	Riders of Judgment
1959	Conquering Horse
1961	Arrow of Love (stories)
1962	Wanderlust* (trilogy)
1964	Scarlet Plume
1965	The Secret Place**
1966	Winter Count (poems)
1966	King of Spades
1968	Apples of Paradise (stories)
1968	Eden Prairie
To Be Released	Milk of Wolves

* A new revised version of a work that was originally published in three separate volumes, *The Primitive*, *The Brother*, and *The Giant*.

** Originally published as *The Man Who Looked Like the Prince of Wales*; reprinted in paperback as *The Secret Place*.

Arnold John Dyson-77-

Publisher's Preface

Early in 1964 John R. Milton, then Chairman of the Department of English, University of South Dakota, conducted these conversations with Frederick Manfred in the Vermillion studios of KUSD–TV. The thirteen Manfred–Milton video tapes were the first in a series of conversations with Western American novelists which now form an extensive film library available on request to educational television stations.

Dr. Milton made the next group of programs with Frank Waters in the fall of 1964, and over the next several years conducted talks with Michael Straight, Max Evans, Vardis Fisher, Arlene Zekowski and Stanley Berne, and William Eastlake. Audio tape conversations with Walter Van Tilburg Clark, Harvey Fergusson, and Wallace Stegner completed the series in the summer of 1969.

Dr. Milton's conversations with Straight, Evans, and Fisher were published by Dakota Press (Vermillion, S. D., 1970) in a single volume entitled *Three West*; the *Conversations with Frank Waters* have been published by Swallow Press (Chicago, 1973).

Conversations with Frederick Manfred was filmed in a two-and-a-half-day period. Mr. Manfred says,

I had an idea that the series would go pretty good, so I warned the director, Ernest Phelps, to have plenty of tapes ready, that we might make as many as a half-dozen tapes in one day. As it turned out, we did six the first day, four the second day (they did run out of tapes that second day when I was all set to do seven), and three the third day. The only break we took was the time it took to replace the tapes. That's why the series looks as if it were done all in one blast. It even builds up to a kind of climax.

Reading the transcriptions now some ten years later, I can see where John and I had some pretty good exchanges. Though here and there it is evident that my memory, and my thinker, and even my maker, weren't always at their best. But I guess you can't have good luck all the time. Overall it's still better this way than if we'd made thirteen carefully planned and carefully canned half-hour television shows.

Mr. Manfred edited the typescript transcribed from the video tapes and added the footnotes signed FFM; the publisher's footnote additions are in brackets.

Throughout the book Dr. Milton's comments are set in italic type and Mr. Manfred's in roman.

Foreword by Wallace Stegner

Writing is the absorbing purpose of Fred Manfred's life, and few Americans have made so ambitious an effort to create a fictional world that extends through space and time. Only William Faulkner and Wright Morris — and in an odd, fantastic way James Branch Cabell — have made a fictional country, and peopled it, and given it a history as Manfred has. Nevertheless it is hard to think of him in the ordinary way as a writer. Writing is only one aspect of him, a by-product of his enormous energy. He is as tall as a South Dakota windmill, and such winds howl through his scaffolding, and his blades spin and groan with such a violence of driven metal, that the stream of fictional water he brings up from underground seems almost insignificant by comparison with the overwhelming machinery that produces it.

He is not a writer in the usual sense. He is a natural force, related to hurricanes, deluges, volcanic eruptions, and the ponderous formation of continents. As one hears of his family, it seems less a family than a primitive horde — five brothers, nine stepsisters and a stepbrother, countless aunts and uncles and cousins, and receding files of ancestors, all nine feet tall, full of Beowulfian laughter, and with voices like the Bull of Bashan. He has not *descended* from his Frisian ancestors, moreover; he has poured into the present like floodwater from a ruptured dam.

His conversations with John Milton indicate that at least in some moods he takes pride in the realism of his fiction. He believes, for instance, that *Riders of Judgment* is a realistic cowboy novel, a reasonably faithful recreation of the historical Johnson County War. Without depreciating his research among the relatives and friends of Nate Champion, I do not believe him for a minute about the realism of that book, or any of the Buckskin Man books. Reality is too small for him. Before he ever started digging into the facts of Nate Champion's life and death, Champion was a hero to him, a Hector, and it was as hero that he fired Manfred's imagination. In fact, all the principal characters in the books that most express Fred Manfred are larger than life, culture heroes half-translated already into constellations in the heavens. Look at old Hugh Glass. Look at He Comes from Conquering a Horse.

The movement of Fred Manfred from reality and history to myth is as inevitable as the expansion of gas to fill an empty space. He writes best about authentic heroes, not about the obscure farm boys he grew up among. He equates the early experience of the American West, and especially of that chosen country he calls Siouxland, with the actions of Homeric Greece or the Iceland of the sagas. Only the heroic stretches him to his full length. In his more truly realistic fiction, for example the lugubrious Dust Bowl novel *The Golden Bowl*, or the humorous *Chokecherry Tree*, or the semiautobiographical trilogy *Wanderlust*, or the compact and wistful *Secret Place*, Manfred strikes me as writing in hobbles. Something — the reduction and tameness of the contemporary world, a tradition of Midwestern commonplace that he obeys without conviction — hampers and limits him. He can't get as excited about his Maurys and his Elofs as he can about any variety of the Buckskin Man. They don't let him rise up and bestride Siouxland like a colossus the way his Indians and Mountain Men and cowboys do. "I like to be wide awake," he tells John Milton, and he is. His nickname for one of the people who half represent him in the realistic fiction is "Free." But Free in contemporary Siouxland is altogether smaller in stature than Hugh Glass or Conquering Horse or even Cain Hammett in the wide open spaces of the past.

Reality is not the only thing that is too small for Fred Manfred. The English language and at least some of the conventions of literature are too small too. Because he does not like the word "novel," he invents a thing called a "rume," a coinage that I do not think will take. His impatience with linguistic patterns leads him into frequent neologisms, whose effect on the dramatic illusion is approximately that of a splinter on a nylon stocking. He wrenches and shoves at his verbs, forcing them into a kind of locoed vigor that in the end defeats his purpose by calling attention to itself. He likes to use adjectives as adverbs, with the same result. And he hangs extravagant names or nicknames on some of his people, for example on the cowboys of *Riders of Judgment*. He is perfectly right about the prevalence of the nicknaming habit among cowboys, but he hasn't heard them right. His Stuttering Dick, Long Guts Everding, Dried Apple Bill, and Peakhead Jim are out of Bret Harte, not out of authentic cow country. You cannot hear them as names uttered by men's mouths.

Reality is too small for him, language is sometimes too arthritic for his needs, and his efforts to loosen and enlarge them are not uniformly successful. He is a very tall man who can never learn to duck to the doors of habitual humans and keeps cracking his head.

He is not as free of entanglement in the Western myths as his remarks to John Milton would suggest: there is no iconoclast in him. Nor is he, despite his verbal rebellions, a technical innovator. The structure and technique of his novels are completely orthodox, even conventional. Moreover, the experience he records, whether out of the buckskin past or the clodhopper present, is essentially parochial, and he has never achieved any great aesthetic distance in his rendering of it: he has only insisted that the local can be universal. Of course it can. But the literary critic might want to suggest that the experience of pitch is better rendered by a fly who has escaped it and sits outside of it than by one who is stuck in it up to the wing-joints.

In his conversations with Milton, Manfred suggests that I am probably not regional enough — I haven't made up my mind whether I am East or West. He is right, in a sort of way. Let us say that I would prefer not to be limitedly either, and regret to see writers I admire patrolling merely regional frontiers. On reading and rereading Manfred I have sometimes wished that he were not as regional as he rather belligerently is. The very concentration on Siouxland that gives him his strength is also, it seems to me, a limitation in that he has nothing to compare it with, he does not see it from outside. To try to create a province, I believe, is a good thing, but not so good a thing as to try to create a world.

These remarks I make descriptively, not in the way of literary criticism. Writers ought to stick together against the arrogance of critics, whose function is too often to whittle a writer down to the critic's size. I have no desire to whittle Fred Manfred down. I like him the size he is, or even bigger, and I would like to see him judged, not by devotees who admire everything he does simply because it *is* regional, and not by provincials from New York who haven't the slightest notion of what he is talking about, but by fellow writers and fellow Westerners who do understand what he is doing and do feel the pull of his materials. That they may have different notions of how to do certain things, and a different linguistic and cultural and historical emphasis, will not much matter.

The important thing for any literary criticism to recognize, if it takes on Fred Manfred, is that his best effects are all big. He paints with a broom and carves with an axe, and his monuments are meant to be viewed at a distance of fifty miles.

Probably he will come after me in war paint for saying what I am about to say, and I will have to flee across country wider and more dangerous than that over which Hugh Glass crawled. I will have to travel by night and never sleep within a mile of my fire, I will have to hide in beaver houses, I will have to submerge among the tules and breathe through a reed. But I think I will risk it anyway, and try to express Fred Manfred as he seems to one who likes and admires him, takes him seriously, and shares a good many of the cultural inheritances, assumptions, and experiences from which he operates.

He seems to me a gigantic and gifted primitive, intelligent, vastly energetic, pretty much self-educated. In the same spirit of friendly disagreement in which he thinks me not regional enough, I think him a shade too provincial in his point of view. He is as independent as a hog on ice, and knowing who he is and what he wants to do, he will properly pay no attention to what I think. He boils with imaginative vigor and a mighty gusto — loves people, country, action, color — and he trusts his Old Lizard more than I would trust mine. He is steeped in the life, both past and present, of the country he grew up in, and is dedicated to recreating it in fiction. As I have indicated, he seems to me more successful in his historical and more romantic fiction than in his realistic stories of contemporary farm and town people: the very fact that he calls his chosen country Siouxland rather than Cornland or Hogland is an indication of where his imagination hankers. And yet he has an inclination, too, to defend his farm boys and middle-class townspeople as legitimate figures of fiction; he *asserts* them into the teeth of a critical climate inclined to recognize neither the West nor realism.

No hairsplitter, no historian of fine consciences, he is a little rough in both his realistic and romantic phases, but he compensates for his roughnesses of surface by an extraordinary vigor. He is forever chanting his Whitmanesque celebration of hope, heroism, and high purpose. He has indeed kept every door open, as he tells John Milton he wants to. He would agree with William Dean

Howells that nothing that God has made is contemptible. And in all his six feet nine inches there is not a quarter inch of fashionable cynicism or malaise. When he admits to being tempted by the Paul Bunyan story one instantly sees why.

Few writers ever achieve so sure a sense of place, and of how human beings are shaped by it. He is the reverse of the nature-fakers; he knows his country from the anthills up. His story of how he prepared himself to write about the Crawl of Hugh Glass is typical: I wish I had been a sparrow hawk, to hover above that monument of a man as he crawled up a stony hill, dragging one leg, pushing his nose among the curly grass, tasting ants to see how they might strike the palate of a broken and starving and in-domitable Mountain Man.

On people he is less sure than on place, though he is endlessly curious and open about them. He seems to me best on the heroic and mythic ones and on those who, like Free, reflect a substantial part of himself. Less good, sometimes forced to an excess of idio-

syncrasy, are some of the minor "realistic" characters such as Elof's father in *The Chokecherry Tree*. What he does have in place of great psychological penetration is variety. The inside of Fred Manfred's head is like the fairgrounds on the Fourth of July. Everybody is there, wide awake and alive.

Finally, Manfred has the indispensable gift that is so frequently dispensed with by contemporary novelists. He can tell a story — start it and keep it rolling like a runaway stagecoach in a horse opera until it crashes in whatever canyon or against whatever cliff he has prepared for it. A reader, once things have been set in motion under him, can do nothing but hang on. I must carefully state, in self-defense in case Fred Manfred is now after me with tomahawk in hand for my quibbling, that I thought up my quibbles after the crash, not during the ride. I was hanging on and being thrilled by the ride through book after book.

That tension and excitement is present whether he is writing or talking. I might want to argue now and then, being an argumentative type, but I would ride a long way to get involved in Fred Manfred's talk, and when his geyser finally fell from a burst to a simmer, I would most certainly have the feeling I have after reading his talks with John Milton: that I have been somewhere, in a real presence, blown around and tossed by an elemental force.

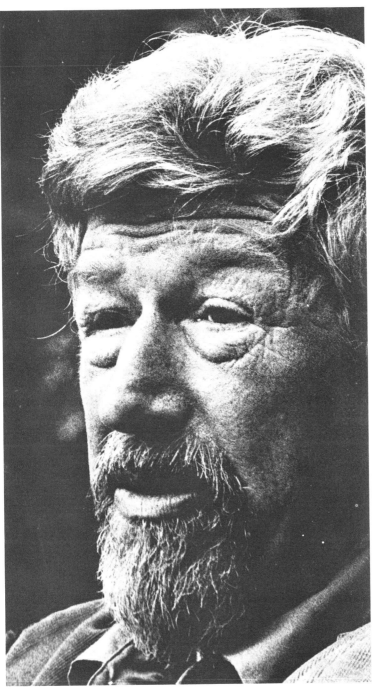

Photo by John Dziadecki. Logan, Utah, June 1972.

Conversations . . .

Milton: About the name "Feikema" which you used — what were the years again?

Manfred: 'Forty-four through 'fifty-one. Nineteen fifty-one was the year I added Manfred legally.

But the first book that the name Manfred was on was Lord Grizzly.

That was 'fifty-four.

It has been ten years at least now since Manfred has been on the books . . . in public.

That's right.

Feikema seems to be a good writing name for an author, and now I see the publishers refer to it as a pen name. So you thought it was a good name for a certain period. Why did you drop it?

Well, there were a lot of reasons. People consistently mispronounced it, which disturbed me. A professor up here in Sioux Falls swears up and down that the correct way to pronounce it is "Fee'-ka Fee-key'-ma," and he, of all people, should have been the one to know how to pronounce it. I was actually baptized Frederick Feikema. There was a big fight about the first name Frederick when I was born, between my folks and my great uncles. Had I been born in the old country, as my grandfather was, my name would have been Feike Feikes Feikema VII.

Did your father go by the sixth?

Yes, in the Feikema genealogical tree in The Netherlands he is down as the sixth. I have this tree thing at home now. Some engineer relative living in Hengelo, The Netherlands, worked it all out. The tree is tremendously broad at the base and goes out in all directions. I am the direct descendant somehow.

For seven generations each first child was a boy, and I, of course, as the oldest born, was a boy. But my father, and my grandfather also, felt that we were Americans and that we shouldn't have these old-country names. When Grandpa came to this country at the . . . is it at Ellis Island that you land? . . . they asked his name and he gave it as Feike Feikes Feikema V. They threw up their hands and said, "You can't have that in America." They asked him where he was from, and even there he had to give a piece of misinformation in a sense. The Hollanders called our old home town Franeker, when actually in Frisian it is Frjentsjer. But he gave it as Franeker, and they said, "Oh. Frank. Your name here in America will be Frank Feikema." That is what they put down at Ellis Island. They didn't change the whole name. Actually this is a funny thing, since the Frisians had a deep-seated dislike of the Franks. They fought so often with them and lost. Charles the Hammer and Charles Pepin defeated them in battles along the Rhine River and so the Frisians have always hated the Franks. To call a Frisian a Frank, even though it was just a name, is still the wrong thing. But Grampa accepted it and my dad took that first name also—Frank.

Are there any Frisians left in Europe, or are all the Frisians in Michigan and Iowa?

No, most Frisians still live in Europe. And there are many Frisians in Iowa. Many of the American Frisians are changing their names. From Heerema to Herman. The people called Boon call themselves either Boone or Bean, which is a good translation. They are gradually learning how to adjust. In the case of my grandfather . . . there is an interesting tale . . . he was a little different from most of the Frisians who came over here. Most of them are religious, Dutch Calvinist, so they go to a Dutch church. So while they speak the Frisian at home, they usually listen to Dutch sermons in the Dutch churches. That's their nearest church tie. Nowadays, of course, the sermons are all American, or English, whichever way you want to look at it. My grandpa was a little on the wild side. You see, his grandfather's grandfather, the first Feike, was a man of property, who owned a big farm called Groot Lankum just outside Franeker. There was a landed gentry in Friesland and he was probably one of their leaders in Franeker.

But somewhere around 1760 the pestilence cleaned him out. He lost all his cattle, Friesian-Holstein cows, or Holstein-Friesians, and lost the Frisian horses he had. Wonderful horses. The Frisian horse is a black horse with a very wide hoof so that on that wet land he won't sink in. This is the horse's feature, the wide hoof. The first Feike lost all those, and he also lost his pigs, and so he was thrown on the labor market. As so often happened in the last century, for several generations after they have been dispossessed by misfortune, they will go to church faithfully, almost fanatically.

Just in case it was God who had taken their . . . ?

Yes, maybe it was that too. But it is sort of a solace to go to church. And for several generations they will hang onto their social position with tremendous determination. The fourth or fifth generation they really tip in. They are going down into the laboring classes. But some of them, before that happens, will come to America. This accounts for the fact that so many people who immigrate are very religious, whereas the people who remain in the old country are not so religious. What is the figure — 1 or 2 percent of the people in Denmark are active church members, for example?

Two percent, and the same is true for all the Scandinavian countries.

And the same is true for The Netherlands and Germany. Whereas in this country it is about 45 percent. This is due to this little business of people being dispossessed of some lofty notion of what they once were in life, and, when they no longer had it, they came over here. Well, that's what happened to Grandpa. With this exception, that Grandpa loved what we would say today is America. The folks of his wife-to-be (her maiden name was Ytje Andringa) were wealthy. They would have nothing to do with him, and for a while prevented her from seeing him, so he went to sea. He had gone to school too, grammar school, and was well read. He went all over the world as a sailor, and then on one of his trips back to the old country, as I remember the story, eloped with her. The first place they landed was Grand Rapids, Michigan.[1] There is a real Holland area there. There is a little town by the name of Friesland there too.

Oh, there is?

Just as there is a Friesland in Minnesota, too. Where Frisians settled and tended to congregate. Grandpa was in Grand Rapids, Michigan, one year. Later he said that he got better treatment, that he got better jobs, from the so-called Americans, the worldly people, much oftener, much sooner, than he did from the Hollanders. In fact, he said the Hollanders tended to be offish and hard to get along with. So he wouldn't go to their church. He pretty much cut himself off, as it were. When he finally came out here . . . I go into Grandpa a lot because he was . . . my relatives say that of all his descendants I most resemble him, which accounts for me being what I am . . . kind of a . . . well, I don't go to church much . . . . I have set myself apart somewhat from the Hollanders like he did. So I, therefore, must be a replica of the old gent.

How about size? Does that come from him, or was the whole family big?

No, Grandpa was a short fellow, about five feet six inches. But he was a broad-shouldered man. That generation of Feikemas were short. But there were some Andringas, Gramma Ytje's people, that were seven feet, far back.

Then this came up again in your generation?

Yes. Though my mother's people are tall too. And broad-shouldered. Well, anyhow, Grandpa then . . . to tell you the story shortly . . . then homesteaded near Perkins Corner (across the border in Iowa here) a couple of years, then traded the place in for a section of land in South Dakota which turned out to be in what is now the Badlands National Monument.[2] He came back out of that broke. With some cactus. We still have some of that cactus.

[1] Actually, I learn later, at Orange City, Iowa, first, and then Grand Rapids. FFM

[2] Actually, his stopping places in America were Orange City, Iowa; Grand Rapids, Michigan; Perkins, Iowa; Lebanon, Missouri; Doon, Iowa; somewhere in the Badlands, Dakota; and finally again, Doon, Iowa. FFM

He landed in Doon, Iowa, where he worked both as a stonemason and on the section for the Old Omaha. He used to help the IWW's up and down the track as he felt sorry for them and gave them rides on his little handcar. Which you pump up and down. He was known to never go to church. My grandma (his wife) died and his family broke up. Aunt Kathryn landed with some people of New England descent in Doon. My father did too. My father really was raised not as a Hollander, nor as a Frisian, but as an American. He was a member of the Congregationalist Church and was raised in a New England family. Almost as their son. George Pohlman. Later in the Ed Harming and the Reynolds families. They were all of New England descent. Dad is now married for the third time and he, wonderfully enough, married a woman who comes from New England, so he has made the complete circle. That was Dad's people. West Frisian they were. Frisians. I might go into that. The Frisians. If you will check the encyclopedia, will check into Old English history, you will find they were probably the original Anglo-Saxons. There were at one time five related tribes: Angles, Saxons, Frisians, Jutes, and Wends. From the Jutes we get the name Jutland way up in the top of Denmark. The Wends disappeared. No one really knows what happened to them. They probably went back East. All of the Anglo-Saxon people originally, it is believed, came, far back, from an area near Lithuania. That's probably where they first originated. The Wends went back in that direction and may have become either the Slovenes or the Slovaks, scholars are not quite sure. The Wends were probably overrun by Slavs, all the men killed off and the women and children kept. Women carry some of the language and some of the customs, so there is where the word either "vak" or "vene" would come in. But "slo" would be from the Slav male side, "Slovak" and "Slovene." The Angles and Saxons lived inland a ways. And the Frisians occupied the Frisian Islands and the mainland called Friesland today in The Netherlands, in Germany, and in Denmark. When it became overpopulated the Frisians had a rule, that is, Magna Frisia (this included the Angles and Saxons) had a rule that a lottery be held. And it was always obeyed, without having to use any force. Each community had its "thing" (where we'd say assembly). And the "allthing" or parliament was held on Helgo-

land, sacred to the Frisians. (The English bombed it because the Germans put some submarine nests in there in the Second World War. And in the First World War too, I understand.) Every year the Frisian leaders met at the allthing on Helgoland, or Holy Land, and there they would decide if the land was overpopulated. They would hold what they called a lottery. The heads of the families would meet and they would have to draw slips of paper . . . no, it was done by little sticks . . . and every tenth family that got the short stick would have to go. This is where the expression "That is my lot" comes from. And so every so often a group of Frisians would emigrate. But it wasn't going fast enough for the Angles and Saxons, as I understand it . . . . Some of this is legend, by the way. It hasn't been recorded by historians that I know of. It comes down by way of my great uncles.

This is how far back now?

Oh, this is the year I'd say about 500 or 600 A.D. The time of Hengest and Horsa. The Frisians had the boats (they were boatmakers and sailors) and so the Frisians transported them to England, brought the Angles and Saxons over in what we now speak of as the Anglo-Saxon invasion. That was the time they ran into King Vortigern, king of the Britons. The Frisians tell a wonderful story about that encounter. King Vortigern wouldn't sell them any land, but he finally agreed to sell them "a hide of land" for their services in helping him fight the Picts and the Scots. So the Frisians very carefully cut up the hide of an ox into a long thin circular strip, around and around and around, and that gave them an acre. You can imagine they cut that quite thin. A hide of land each family was allowed to have. King Vortigern thought that his "hide of land" device would chase them out. It didn't. And in addition he also lost his daughter to one of them. I forget which one, Hengest or Horsa. Now, if you will check through English history . . . even today on an English map you will see that many Frisians immigrated with the Angles and Saxons to the British Isles. Probably saw a pretty Briton girl, one of the sailors, say, and he married her and stayed on, et cetera. But in names like Dumfrieshire, Frisingham, Frisby-on-the-Rye, Frisington, Friston — I checked one day and there was about fifty such place names in

England — you can see the remnants of that Frisian invasion. But there were never quite enough Frisians to give England an overall Frisian stamp. The overall stamp was really English. It was mostly the Angles and Saxons that took hold there.

Since this is just about the time that the English language was being formed as we know it, then is it reasonable to say that Frisian is part of the roots of modern English?

Yes, it is. But ——

Frisian as it would be spoken in Holland would sound something like English?

Old English.

And some of this gets into your writing, no doubt?

Oh, yes. That's why it was rather marvelous to discover. Reared on the farm out in the country you've got one strike against you. I mean as against the city boys. By a city I mean a city of five hundred. In those days Doon was the biggest town around. You've got one strike against you as a clodhopper. Then in addition to that, I was a Frisian. The Frisians were a minority group within the Holland group. The Holland Dutch church.

Christian Reformed now.

In other words, I had two strikes against me. I came from a minority group within a minority group. The Hollanders themselves are a minority group within the American society. So I went through my early life with these weights on my shoulders. And yet at the same time what kept the leaven alive in me was the fact that Grandpa felt he was an American first of all. He wouldn't . . . he never spoke the Dutch language again after arriving in America. He knew the minority group problem. Because he was born in Dutch Friesland. (He did speak some Frisian, however, with his mother in America, in private, but he did so reluctantly.) He immediately learned to speak the English or American language upon arriving in America, and I, and others tell me this too, never heard a single sound in his inflection that would tell you that he was a foreigner. Perfect English.

> *Weren't others speaking Frisian in the Doon community though?*

Oh, yes, among the Feikema relatives, they all did. And then there were some other Frisian families there. And my father spoke Frisian at home. And my uncles did. I spoke Frisian as a little boy, a little bit. And of course English. It wasn't until I was in college. . . . And another thing, I was very huge. I grew very fast and very rapidly. At the age of twelve, when I started high school, I was almost as big as some of the seniors, who in those days were some twenty years old. But I wasn't, of course, as strong. I was slender, thin, awkward. Had big feet and hands, with little or no muscles. Just bones. I was kind of a weird sight. I used to think of myself as an Ichabod Crane a lot. I felt great sympathy for old Ichabod. (I thought that was a great story, by the way.) I liked a girl named Katinka too, like he did.[3] She was my cousin, which I wasn't supposed to like, and all that sort of stuff. . . . I was in college when I was given an assignment in an English course where I had to read some Chaucer. College (Calvin College) was in Grand Rapids, Michigan. To my great astonishment I could read Chaucer, except for the few imported French words that came by way of Normandy. One day I was asked to read it aloud. The prof, you know, he liked to challenge the class now and then, and he asked them to read this strange Chaucer, and when it came my turn, I read it the way a Frisian would read it. His eyes instantly lit up and he said, "Ah, class, that is the true way to read it. Even my way is wrong." You see, I had the Frisian accent in there. The first two lines . . . how do they go now? . . . "Whan that Aprille with his shoures sote/ The droghte of Marche hath perced to the rote" . . . that's the Frisian way. By the way, I might give you two lines of Frisian. The Frisians had a shibboleth (do you remember that expression from the Bible?) to detect the enemy, to see if they could pronounce it correctly. The Frisians had a big war with the Hollanders one time. A Holland spy would

---

[3] Actually, named Katherine. FFM

sneak across the line sometimes and try to pick up their plots and plans. The way the Frisians would detect the Hollanders was to have them repeat these two lines: "Buter, brea, en griene tsiis, hwa thit net sizze kin, is gjin oprjuchte Fries," which translated means "Butter, bread, and green cheese, who that cannot say, is not a true (or upright) Frisian." The word upright (*oprjuchte*) means true. It probably means, in a sense, up right, to stand a straight true man. And it was on the word *oprjuchte* that the stranger stumbled . . . . Now to speak of my mother's people. An interesting tale there. I have always been a little suspicious of it except that there is some evidence that it probably is true. The story goes something like this. There was a man named Hermann von Engen[4] who, somewhere in about 1865, was the baron or the head man of a principality, or what we might say was a county, a territory, in northwest Germany. He was the head guy there. When Bismarck amalgamated Germany and made it one state, this guy Hermann bucked. He didn't want any part of this. He wanted to keep his old feudal setup there. He was doing fine. He had a couple of wives. And maybe some concubines nobody knew about. It's always curious that there is in every one of those little principalities one stamp on them all. They all have the same kind of nose, the same kind of cleft smile, et cetera. One guy probably sires a good many of each generation, what with first-night rights and so on. They all look alike when you see them. You can instantly recognize his stamp when you see one.

He'd have trouble marrying any Frisian then.

All would be cousins over there. Old Bismarck booted him out and he escaped across a thing called the Dollart — it's a little bay coming down from the North Sea between East Friesland in Germany and Drenthe in The Netherlands. He escaped with his wife, with my grandfather Frederick, who was then a baby, and an older son, and a girl.[5] They lived in Drenthe one

[4] According to my Uncle Hank, Henry Van Engen of Hull, Iowa, "Engen" might have been spelled with the letter "l." Just how, he couldn't say. "Lengen"? "Englen"? FFM

[5] I have just returned from the old country (3–4–1974) and have finally got the Van Engen business straightened out. It took Pastor Heinrich Volkers of Emlichheim, Hannover, West Germany, my second cousin Henrikus Elders of

Gees, Drenthe, The Netherlands (his father was my mother's full cousin on her mother's side), and myself several days of careful searching through old leather-bound church records in Emlichheim to luck onto the trail. The first day we traced a line of Van Engens from Jan Hendrik Van Engen (the only notation on him was that he left for Amsterdam in 1778) to Harm Van Engen, 1774–1814, to Berend Van Engen, 1801– ?, to Harm Van Engen, 1834– ?. That last Harm's date of birth puzzled me since according to our American version of the Van Engen family tree he should have been born in 1822. Look as we might we couldn't find anything more that first day. We did determine, though, that they were all landbouwers, owning a farm called Woeste Huise (house in a waste place). Hendrik Elders and I found Woeste Huise and discovered it was a considerable farm surrounded by peat bogs and swamp with only one road out of it. We next stopped at Coevorden (near Gees, Drenthe) and asked the clerk of the Gemeente (district) Coevorden to see what he could find. He came up with the name of only one Van Engen, my grandfather Frederik, born June 6, 1861. The date was right but the place wrong. Our family tree shows him born in Emlenkamp (now Emlichheim). The clerk at Coevorden became intrigued in the problem and after we left continued his search after work and, at my suggestion, looked through various miscellaneous records. He called us at dinner that night to say he had found what we were after. The next morning we drove over and found that Geert, Aaltien, Jan Hendrik, and Frederik (my mother's father) were all born in Coevorden, not Emlenkamp, that their father Harm Van Engen was born in Emlenkamp, Hannover, in 1882, and their mother Aaltien Peters was born in Wilsum, Hannover, in 1826. We crossed the border again to see Pastor Volkers. Once more we got out the old leather record books. We couldn't find Harm Van Engen listed in the 1822 file. I decided to page back through the 1821 and 1820 files. And there it was, Harm Van Engen, born in 1820. Further, there was a notation stating that he was the son of a Geert Van Engen, who upon marrying Fenne Swiers Van Engen, widow of the Harm Van Engen born in 1774 and deceased in 1814, changed his name from Geert Albers to Geert Van Engen. The notation further stated this was done to keep the place known as Woeste Huise in the Van Engen name. Geert Albers was listed as a "jongmann" (young man or hired hand). He *was* young. His date of birth given on their wedding day was 1787, but in another place was given as 1792. The date of the wedding was 1816. This made Widow Fenne thirty-six years old and Geert either thirty or twenty-five. Later, Widow Fenne's first child by Harm Van Engen, Berend Van Engen, 1801– ?, married in 1833 and had a son in 1834. This son was also named Harm. Berend's wife died the next year from tuberculosis, and Berend did not remarry. The district records for the years 1848–1851 are missing. By 1851 Widow Fenne was in her seventies. We couldn't find the year she died either before or after those three years, so we presumed she died during that interval. It is also about that time that the Harm born in 1820 must have married Aaltien Peters, because suddenly he took up residence with his wife in Coevorden on May 1, 1851. Aaltien Peters had the right to wear a gold headband (*goudene oorijzer*), which suggests she came from one of the best families. It is tempting to speculate on what might have happened. When Widow Fenne died, Berend, with his son Harm born in a direct line (1834), ordered the first Harm (1820) off the premises, even if he had married a "rich girl." The great expectations of the 1820 Harm were abruptly shattered and he had to fly with his wife across the border into The Netherlands. There may have even been a fight between the thirty-year-old Harm and the fifty-year-old Berend. Perhaps Berend asked the law to chase him off. Gramma always said they had to fly in a boat across some water (over the river Aa which drains that vast swampy land and which in May could have been out of its banks?). In generation — let's say twenty years. And with them escaped another couple of families, probably retainers or related to them. At any rate, during the twenty years they stayed in The Netherlands, they picked up one eighth Drenthe blood and one eighth Holland blood, so three fourths is East Frisian. That one eighth Drenthe is really ancient Saxon. Curiously enough, the Frisians have a nickname for the people of Drenthe, "Smoargje Drintsk," which means "dirty Drenthe." What that really meant in the old days was someone very lusty and hearty who liked to eat fatty meat. They eat a lot of fat and they live sort of in a very earthy lusty manner. Actually this is the characteristic of the old Anglo-Saxons, of the old ancient Saxons.

This explains Chaucer.

Chaucer and all his lusty stuff. And it explains me too. Though a Frisian tends at first to be a little gruff — until you get to know him. Because he fights the seas for months at a time and learns to conserve his energy. Until he gets home. Then he lets go. At any rate it was great for me to learn that I was first of all not only an American as my grandfather and my father always tried to tell me, but that I also had a lot of Old English blood in me. This had a lot to do later on with the changing of my name, or adding Manfred to it. The name Frederick, by the way, came from my mother's father, whose name was Frederick. He was known as Frederick Van Engen in this country. It happens that when I was going to be published for the first time I had quite an argument with my publisher about my name. He said, "What shall the name be?" I said, "I'd like to have an American name." I felt like an American. And furthermore I had a lot of Old English blood in me. "This old Frisian should have a name that's in keeping with the language. I wouldn't mind if I were of some other descent, but it just happens I'm very Old Anglo-Saxon and I don't see why I shouldn't have a name that reflects that. There's no harm

any case, the people living in the district of Coevorden, The Netherlands, and the people living in the district of Emlichheim are all Saxons. Both speak pretty much the same language. They visit back and forth across the border without being challenged. My cousin Henrikus and I were waved across both times without examination of passports. Thus it now appears I am half Frisian and half Saxon. FFM in that. Not any more than, say, if I had a Jewish name or an Italian name. Or Indian name like Youngblood." "No," he said, "that's right. But," he said, "I like your last name Feikema because it's different. And the nickname your family called you, 'Feike,' (which is what the Feikema relatives still call me — I am the firstborn of the firstborn of the firstborn, the "stamhalder," I am "the Feike") I'd like you to use that." And that is why the first five, six, no, seven books of mine were printed under the name of Feike Feikema. I always felt, though, that that name was sort of artificial. And I have always felt that it was kind of like a pen name. My mother called me Frederick, rarely called me Fred or Feike. Always Frederick. Two of my dearest friends always called me Frederick too. Which I liked. I was Fred to everybody else. So when I discovered through Professor Konstantin Reichardt, who is now in the foreign language department, I understand, at Yale . . . when Reichardt was at the University of Minnesota, he once asked a mutual friend if he could meet me, because he had never met a Frisian. He wanted to ask me some questions about the Frisian people. He loved the old languages. I asked him one day if he wouldn't find out for me what the name "Feike" meant. Well, in about a week I had a letter from him saying that from old manuscripts, as far as he could make out, "Feike" came from the same root as did "Frederick," "freedom," and something else . . . I forget what that is . . . "Friday" came from. The root was "pri-tu." It went back at least two thousand years. Originally the name was "Friducho," both for "Feike" and "Frederick." In the case of "Feike," by the process of petnaming, "Friducho" was shortened to "Friccho," then "Friccho" became "Ficco," and "Ficco" became "Feike" . . .

. . . The idea for *Winter Count* was interesting. I was looking at some pictures of old hides on which the Indians had painted the hieroglyphs of their winter count. The Indians counted by winters. For the calendar year. And while I was looking, I was trying to figure out what each hieroglyph meant, and why a chief would want to do this one instead of another one, et cetera. There was one chief . . . I forget which one, I think it was a Mandan . . . who had a winter count for each year of his life. And it occurred to me: I wonder how I would do it if I were to make a "winter count" of my life. So I began to jot down some things, just the way they fell off the end of my pencil and pen. It looked a little as though it all might be poetry. Or something like it. Well, then I really got hot on it, and I wrote it down pretty much as she wanted to come. I wrote probably three or four of those a day until I had finished eighteen.

Winter Count *is probably the closest you have come to being precisely accurate.*

Before that I have done the usual . . . well, I won't say distortion of, but invention on, autobiographical material.

Are all of your brothers still living?

Yes. Ed, the second one, the one that's next to me (I am the oldest) Ed is in Doon. Near Doon on a farm. He's a bachelor. Floyd is an executive with a mortgage firm in Minneapolis, and doing very well. As we say in America, successful. A good job and so on. A little hard to take once in a while, because he always knows the exact answer when it comes to money problems, and what's wrong with me that I haven't made a couple of million, et cetera. When that's about the last thing I think of. That is, that comes about fourth or fifth. I think of other things first. Let's see, next is John. John is in California. He owns sort of a garage and filling station. He is a mechanic. All the Feikemas are good mechanics. I am supposed to be the worst; though, even so, I am fairly good. The truth is that I am really quite good, but I haven't paid any attention to it. It's only when I need to that I call it forth. I am too busy with other things. Then, there is Abben. He is also very mechanically minded. I have always thought that Abben was very bright. But the war came along and he went to CCC Camp, then into the Navy, and was in the war for . . . actually he was in since before Pearl Harbor and all the way through until 'forty-six. He was in on some wild times. He was on some of those mother ships, carriers, and he lost one under him. He couldn't swim but he somehow survived. Landed in some jungle somewhere. He wrote a diary about some of this, but the Navy took it away from him, which I have always sort of bitterly resented. I would like to have kept that. They may still have it and someday, if I become power-ful enough, I'll walk into the War Department and ask for it, be-cause I could surely use it. Any secrecy they might have to have had then should surely be washed away by now.

> *Oh, yes. Everyone is publishing diaries of the war now.*

Sure. He was a mechanic in the Navy and was very good. He took care of the VIP airplanes. He is still in the Navy Reserve. And he was also what they call "a man who looked for lemons" in the Buick division, listening to see what's wrong. And then if he found a lemon, he was supposed to take it out and determine how it came about. He has now quit that job though and is going back to college. And has found that he has a very good mind. So my instinct was right about his mind. He is enjoying it very much. Warm and wonderful fellow. And to me highly civi-lized. At least to this extent, that he is a perfect set-up for a schem-ing person. He is vulnerable to all these fellows who have quick stick-'em-for-something minds. Some people say you aren't grown up until you know how to make a living and take care of yourself. I say it is still actually an adolescent stage when you know how to make money. When you become truly civilized you become a little like Schweitzer. You live for higher things.

> *If he is that innocent he is likely to become a writer too.*

No, he doesn't have any impulse to write. He really doesn't know what he wants to do. He was a pretty good singer, he might be good in music. I don't know. You mention the word innocent ——

That was going to lead me to another question. Are all of your brothers still named Feikema? They didn't change their names?

No.

Are they as big as you are?

They are all over six-two. Ed is almost as tall as I, Floyd six-six plus, and Abben and John are around six-two and a half. Henry, the youngest, who is a lawyer in one of the Twin Cities and who was with the Attorney General's office for a long time and who now is on his own, he is six foot five. He actually is probably the most gifted in letters, in cultural matters. He catches onto things very rapidly. I always claim the reason he became a lawyer was because he was the youngest. For him to survive he had to learn to play one brother against the other.

Argue his case in the family.

That's right, argue his case and fight. All the more so when my dad remarried. In the second marriage we suddenly had nine stepsisters and one stepbrother. They were most of them older so Henry really had a double shock with all those older ahead of him. So for him to survive he had to learn to measure his words, learn the motivations of people around him, and then steer his way through all of this. He in many ways though is also a type of innocent man.

What I was wondering is, if you are enough of a misfit, or considered yourself enough different from not only the people in the community but also within your family, do you turn to writing somewhat introspectively? Or, you have also mentioned an Aunt Kathryn who taught you in school, is she more of an influence than the social conditions?

There are many influences. I often smile when I read biography. Of course, when you write biography you have to pull some things up and get them encompassed in something like three hundred pages, four hundred, or whatever you are going to do.

Yes.

So you keep throwing things out. But the real truth is, it is actually a thick fabric of various influences, notions, et cetera . . . I suppose I was a misfit in some ways. I remember they had a terrible time taking a picture of me even as a child. We have a picture of me when I was nine months standing by a chair and I am already glowering at the camera.[1] Now where did I learn that? — That's instinctive. That's almost animal. Like taking a picture of a mink. Or a busy cub. You know. He isn't going to stand up to the camera either in a pleasant manner. And it went all the way through my life. The fact that you got me here is sort of a miracle because I still have trouble looking at myself in a mirror or looking at my pictures.

Does a camera represent society?

Well, it's kind of an intrusion. At least in my case, I have a terrible . . . not terrible . . . a strong sense of identity. Who I am, and what my rights are, and what my territory is. Something like a dog. You know, he has his little outposts too that he checks every day. And if any other dog invades that, or even looks at it, he barks at him. Well, I think I bark at people too who invade my area. I have a stronger sense of that than anyone else in our family. I was the oldest son, and living in the country I grew up at first with nothing around me to play with but a dog. My best friend was a dog. We ran off a couple of times together. Once he suggested it and once I did. That was before I started school. But there was a strong sense of being alone and apart. Aunt Kathryn

---

[1] The "glowering" picture actually was taken when I was three years old, when Grandpa Frederick was dying. I was smiling in the picture taken when I was eight–nine months old. FFM

had a lot to do with that and so did my mother. My mother was, as I look back now, an extraordinary woman. She didn't have a line of guile in her. She always knew when the storekeeper took her, but she never started out with the notion that he would take her. And it was always a continual source of amazement to her that it could continue to happen. She thought that it would just happen once. That once he slipped. But the next time he would be okay. She was very warm. She and I spent a lot of time playing games together. I loved music. (We didn't know until much later in my life that I had some musical ability.) My mother was very musical and we spent a lot of time playing riming games together. There would be a sound, and I would try and rime it, and then she would rime mine, and this went on and on. And then Kathryn, who was my father's sister . . . she's a tall asthenic woman and inclined to the beauties of life and not the crudities of life. She tries to avoid and not think of the crudities. Still doesn't. How she managed to exist for some seventy years without really discovering that she is a human animal is beyond me. But she has managed to do this. She is almost pure spirit. Really, it's almost astounding. She lived with us when she was teaching nearby in a country school. One summer just before I was to begin school, she and I were sitting under a cottonwood tree in the northwest corner of the farm grove. She was tatting. You know that stuff where they have an ivory fish about this long and they go in and out like this and embroider or crochet or whatever it is . . . . No, it's tatting. Tatting. In between all these little motions of hers, she said, "Freddie, I don't know what's going to become of you." I didn't pay much attention. I was watching some crickets and a beetle and an ant. I was having my own little fun with the ant world. Then she said, "What are you going to become? What's going to become of you some day?" And her story is that I said, "What's the hardest thing to become?" And she said, "Become a poet." And I said, "Well, that's what I am going to be." This was when I was only about five years old. Or maybe four and a half, something like that. Now that was actually a loaded question on her part. And I call it a loaded question for this reason: she was a schoolteacher and she had also written some poems. The poems were printed by a firm in Sioux City, some hundred copies of them.

We don't have a copy. She has one, but she won't let me see it. I read it when I was a boy, once, but I haven't read it lately, so I don't know how good they are. But she always wanted to be a poetess. Or else a painter. (She also paints fairly well.) So you see that was really a loaded question. Because she had been talking about this poetry around me. So I would naturally respond this way. But of course it is also true that if I really wasn't interested in poetry I would never have said this. I would have said, "I want to be like Pa, a farmer." Or said, "like Uncle so and so, an engineer." Or, "like Grampa, run the railroad." But as it turned out I mentioned writing . . . . About that sense of being alone and apart, it is true that as I grew older, in addition to these other difficulties that I felt were in my life, about being a member of a minority group within a minority group, about being extraordinarily tall and as such overly sensitive and so always had the sensitive side of my nature kept very alive, I also felt that I was somewhat of an orphan in many ways. Intellectually. There were but few books around. Not too many. The Bible was there. My father couldn't read or write. When his mother died he was either eight or nine years old and was sent out to work for these New England people that I mentioned.[2] So, the little learning he had he lost. He can read today if he wants to, but he is too proud to bother with it. And besides, he says, TV has come now and he doesn't need to. He is very good at figures. He knows his figures and he can sign his name. But he couldn't read or write. And I had that in the house. Mother said that she wanted a man to read the Bible at family worship morning, noon, and night. So since I was the oldest boy it fell to me to read the Bible, which was quite early. I read the Dutch Bible first. That is what we heard in church on Sunday and so I learned a little Dutch. Later on I read the Frisian . . . a couple of the Psalms. Then I read the Bible in English. I read the Bible through completely, beginning to end, including all the begats and all the boring stuff, seven times before I was off to college at eighteen.

> *You really started as a reader. The writing, did*
> *that start in college, or did you do some in high*
> *school before entering college?*

[2] Actually, his mother was ill with typhoid fever and for that reason he was sent out to work to earn money for the family. FFM

Oh, no. I began writing before. I would come to grade school with poems and my grade school teacher would . . . . You see, they had some problems with me in grade school too, I guess. The first year I came to school, the primary grade, I was always in trouble. Aunt Kathryn was my teacher the second year and she couldn't keep me busy either. So she immediately stuck me in the first and second grade. Bang! two grades at once. Just to keep me busy. I still got into trouble. Because I remember one day one of the boys caught a field mouse and put it in a Bull Durham sack and pulled the drawstring tight. You know. He wanted to let this loose in school. So I volunteered, because I thought this would be a good joke on Aunt Kathryn. And I did let it go. She was playing the organ, playing "Star-Spangled Banner," you know, and when I let the mouse out, it shot straight for the organ. She got up on the organ chair and screamed her head off. And a little later the neighbor girl, the little Berg girl I think it was, raised her hand and said, "Little Freddie Feikema let that mouse out." My dad laughed that night. But my mother thought that was terrible . . . . I wrote those first poems when I was in the sixth grade. This teacher I had, Aardema, a Frisian, said, "It looks like you are going to be an old-time scribe the way you like to write poems." Then in high school they (my classmates) were so much older than I that I hid the poetic impulses. I did write some love letters which I always burned. I always had a girl. I've had "a girl" in my life as long as I can remember. There was always a favorite girl that I wanted to look at. Even when I was six, seven years old. There's always a girl in my life somewhere, an ideal. You know, Robert Graves calls her the White Goddess.

Someone in the class? A teacher?

Oh, I wasn't a teacher-worshipper. I tended to worship those who were my peers. But they were always in the distance. You see the point of the White Goddess is that you must never touch her. The moment you touch her she is no longer a White Goddess for you. She then is something else. So all those years, not having any sisters, the girls were always off in the distance. But I remember writing little poems to them, and letters in high school, and hid them . . . . I was an insatiable reader, and still am today, can't read enough. In college I was interested in writing, right away. And I had a poem published the second year I was there. I must tell you though that in my freshman year I flunked English.

This has happened to many major writers.

What is it they say? Faulkner never finished high school, took no college courses. Steinbeck never went to college except to audit a course or two. Hemingway didn't either. They didn't get bent by the academic world. I think college (and graduate school) is good for the critical teacher, but if you are creative something goes wrong there even if you have the most marvelous teacher in the world. Something goes wrong in that critical atmosphere of the classroom which discourages the little tiny bud of writing. Thank God that I did flunk English in college, because I knew that I would then be different. I never had really good marks except in courses that I liked. Botany and history. In high school I had marks as high as one could get in history. And everything else was 75.[3]

Now just as you did begin to get serious about writing in college ... you did have basketball. Did that tempt you at all to give up writing? On what basis did you finally make a decision to become a writer instead of a basketball player?

Well, in baseball, I had some scouts following me in baseball. I could throw hard, throw good curves. Possibly the fact that I had the kind of mother that I did, and father, who always stressed the superior values of life, real values . . . . I liked some of the comradery that goes on in baseball games and basketball games. But it never was fully satisfactory. I liked to read a lot. I was offish. They always knew that Fred would be off somewhere reading. I had to hide my first real writings. In high school and college I wrote I guess about ten short stories and a raft of poems. In the beginning I had to hide them from my father. I had a little corner up in the hayloft. You see, he began to sense when I was eight or nine years old that I was drifting away from him. I was his favorite. He loved me very deeply. We are real close today. But

---

[3] A bit exaggerated. Though I was best at history. FFM

we broke apart when I was about eight or nine. That was when he saw that I wasn't going to be like himself. I had this side that he couldn't understand. Here I could read and he couldn't. And I *wanted* to read — this he didn't understand. I was entering a world that absolutely blocked him out. And even if I would try to tell him about it, he would become impatient. I even read to him some. But he became impatient with it anyway. I had to hide all this up in the haymow. I remember when I used to plow that I would hide a book inside my shirt and pants and pull the belt up tight and pull my stomach in and take the horses out to the field, hitch them up, and when I was over the hill I'd hook the lines up on the plow (I had a good lead team), and then I would read to the end, turn around and read until I got to the top of the hill and then hide the book again. This I had to do. I think that resistance is good. I wanted this and they said no to me and this made me feel as if I were an outlander or outsider of the group.

> *And perhaps worked at it a little harder. Now you say that the creative writer is not likely to come out of a college situation. Didn't Calvin College turn out a number of nationally known writers?*

Yes, they did. But every one was a rebel. David Cornel De Jong, a fine first-rate novelist, was a rebel while he was there. He was a scandalous person in the eyes of the Calvinists. Peter DeVries was so brilliant that he just sort of casually went through college. He is a nationally recognized writer today. Satirist. And then there is another one, Meindert De Jong, who is a famous children's writer. I don't think he finished Calvin. They were outcasts on the campus like I was . . . . Later I was one of four fellows eating at the same dining hall table. They called us "the brain trust." That was the wording of the day. The British said, "brains trust," but in America we said "brain trust." Though we had an English-minded professor there who wouldn't say "brain trust." He always said "brains trust". . . . Once I was in some difficulty at Calvin. The reason that I didn't get booted out though, I am sure, was because I wasn't a mean fellow, for one thing. I was kind of tender-hearted. And for another I was on the basketball team. They needed me as a center. So I had a slight hold on them. I remember one night the president was going to kick me off the team, but the coach argued that if they kicked me off then Calvin would go back to its losing ways again. They had to consult their Christian Reformed consciences and finally decided to let me stay on . . . . The first good thing that I wrote, though . . . . You know, I tried all kinds of things. The first good thing I wrote was, "A Harvest Scene." It was written on a day when I shot lonesome for home in memory. I was a junior. My mother was dead; she'd died when I was seventeen. In this memory I went back to Iowa, back to the day when my dad was terribly upset. He'd married the wrong woman and he'd come down with what in those days we called the milkleg. Now we call it undulant fever. I was working for a neighbor to earn some school money, and they called me home to get the harvest in for Dad. And I did it all alone. I harvested some hundred and twenty acres of ripe grain, dead ripe. My brothers changed horses for me, but I just cut night and day until I had all of it cut. Before a storm. I never forgot the beauty of that oncoming storm. So there was this one time when I was lonesome for home at Calvin and I wrote this down. As kind of an impression. Really not for class. But when it was done, I thought, say, this is really not half-bad. I handed it in. The prof got all excited and he made the college paper print it. About that same time too I missed my mother often. She had a tremendous influence on me. Not as much though as my father. My father had the most influence in the long run. Which I thank God for. It's wrong when a son lets his mother put the final stamp on him.

> *You suggested just now that being an outcast or being alone in some ways seems to have something to do with writing. After you left Calvin College did you stay alone for several years?*

Oh, yes. Hitchhiking. Couldn't get jobs. This was the time of the depression. Couldn't get jobs. I had a teacher's life certificate, but . . . I did some practice-teaching, but I hated it. I saw what happened to teachers. They all dried up. Particularly in the closed circuit of the Christian Reformed Church.

For how many years did you hitchhike around the country?

Three.

Where?

Everywhere.

And got quite a lot of material? New experiences?

Oh, yes. A lot of things happened to me. I was picked up one time by the cops, hit over the head, given the Star Chamber business. They thought that I had highjacked a car and when I finally explained who I was and what I was up to, they apologized and picked me up off the floor and brought me out to the road and stopped a car and got me a ride. It was in New Jersey. It was about the time when Hauptmann was being executed.[4] Everybody was tense and the cops were . . . you could see they were on their toes. I tended to be a little slow at speech, to answer questions. I thought of the answer quickly enough, but I didn't know whether I should give it to them. So before I could answer, one guy hit me over the head. They had hard bright lights on me . . . a little like they have here.

You went East first from Calvin, didn't you? Or did you come back here?

No, I went back to the farm first. Then I hitchhiked to Yellowstone National Park. Out of that came a book called *The Golden Bowl*. That was quite an experience. Then I went to Michigan and worked in a warehouse one winter. Part of that wound up in the trilogy. Then I struck out for New York. I landed in New Jersey and worked in a factory there. U.S. Rubber. Then hitchhiked to Washington. Was down there three months trying to get a job. Then I went back to the farm again. Then I went to California and then finally I went to Sioux Falls here for a while and worked in the stockyards as an insurance investigator.

[4] The Bruno Hauptmann thing was in the air all right — but the real factor at work here was that a man had just been killed in New Jersey by a hitch-hiker whom he'd picked up. FFM

And got fired from that because when I learned that farmers were hard up and didn't turn in the right count I couldn't turn them in. I let them go.

> *Well, part of this would be economic. And it also sounds a little bit as though you were on a kind of quest, trying to find yourself, and the country you were going to settle in and write in.*

I was always looking for a town with lakes in it and pretty girls. When I finally hit Minneapolis that really caught my eye. In those days, Minneapolis was beautiful. That was in nineteen thirty-six and 'thirty-seven. It was still a small city. It has become metropolitan now and went commercial.

> *This is partly why you left Minneapolis?*

In some ways, yes. I still really hadn't landed in the right place . . .

. . . Working in the factory wasn't very nice.

Was it as bad for you as it was for Thurs Wraldson in the book Wanderlust*?*

Worse. But I didn't tell about my own private life. The private life I gave to Thurs was something else. My own life was somewhat different. I had some good times, though, in New York. I met a couple of critics. I met a poet who was fairly good, a man named Floyd McKnight who wrote a book called *Buildings*. Pretty good poem. A long poem. Then I went to my first Met performance there, which I had never seen. And I went to the art galleries. And I went wandering around through Greenwich Village. Though I could see that that was pretty decadent. The real Greenwich was gone by the time I got there. There was only a little bit of it left. I guess Max Bodenheim . . . is that his name? . . . was still wandering around. I saw him on several occasions. I wouldn't say that I had anything dramatic happen to me there. It was just that I always felt sort of lonely there. I didn't seem to feel rooted in. And I kept thinking about the plains, even the mountains, the talk and the winds that we have out here, and so I just naturally started drifting west.

It came out just a little bitterly on occasion in the trilogy, and one wonders, you see, whether there was a particular thing that literally drove you out of New York and perhaps later accounted for a certain kind of resentment against what we will call eastern novelists.

Well, possibly. It depends upon which version you are talking about; that is, if it's the old *World Wanderer* first edition of the trilogy or *Wanderlust*.

I was thinking of the first one.

I think in the first one, once I got started on the story I got so involved in how Thurs lived that I probably made up some of the resentments so he would have a few. But my tendency is not to harbor many resentments. I try to live each day complete, and to live it in such a way that I won't regret "yesterday." I can really say, today, that I regret nothing that has ever happened to me. It's all fine with me.

And you have used most of it.

What I have used, I have used, but I haven't really begun to tap it yet.

You have been compared, you know, by some critics, to Thomas Wolfe. What do you think about that?

I can't read him in the first place. He wrote something about a tall man ... I kind of forget ... it was an essay, sixty or seventy pages ... I read that. I try to read each of his novels. I read about thirty or forty pages, and then there is something about it that I don't like. It's too thick and verbose and noisy. I know that if he'd had the training that I have had, sitting on the benches downtown Saturday afternoon, and you shot off your mouth like he did, the old-timers would either push him off the bench or walk away. They wouldn't have any time for him. They like the curt laconic speech which you so often find in Faulkner's narration — not in his exposition, but in his dialogue. You find the laconic there and Hemingway had a lot of this too. That's real Midwest. Perhaps I saw ... maybe this is so, because Wolfe was a huge fellow, and I am supposedly a huge fellow, physically. Maybe there is something to it that I am looking in a mirror. Some people have suggested this to me. To me really, though, that man is artless. He was an artist who was artless.

Sensitive, but little craft.

Now the critics who say this about my things are missing something. Because I do an awful lot of thinking and plotting before I begin a book. I know where the skeleton is and where the flesh is to be attached and the feathers are to go on. When I get done with a book, I like to have it like a pheasant in flight. It works.

It's beautiful. But I know before it flies where every bone and every gut and every feather and every drop of blood and bile and the whole business . . .

Where it is going.

I had it all apart at one time. I think I know why they say it is autobiographical. Because by the time I start to write a book I am so thoroughly the main character that at the time of its creation I *am* this person. And then I do write his autobiography. How can you explain *Conquering Horse*? I wasn't an Indian. And *Lord Grizzly*? I wasn't a Mountain Man. I wasn't anything to begin with in the so-called biographical novels. But, what I do is, I become that character and then I write his autobiography. So it seems that it has that sort of hot intimate feeling of an autobiography. But the truth is that it isn't that.

Which novel does come closest perhaps to being factual? Would that be Boy Almighty?

Yes. But once again I have to tell you that I had a roommate named Howard Anderson who was six-six and who was the son of a very well-to-do family in Minneapolis. They ran the Anderson China Shop on Nicollet Avenue. That's a beautiful place, wonderful place, to go to. Howard and I became very good friends. I tend to be a passive receptor most times. Until I am aroused. Then I am a wild man. But generally I am rather passive for long periods at a stretch. Howard was a fighter. He would fight the nurses, fight the doctor, agitating for this or that. . . . What happened was that I met people on the streets in Minneapolis occasionally who would say, "Hi Fred, how are you?" and they would refer to something that would tell me that I once knew them in the sanatorium. Tuberculosis sanatorium at Oak Terrace. But I couldn't remember them. So I thought: something is going on in my mind that isn't healthy. A callus or a veil or something is growing across my brain and is shutting that whole experience out, and I don't know whether I want that or not. This is a natural thing to do. But not for a writer. He has to keep that all raw so that he can draw from it. Furthermore, I wanted to be a very healthy person and on those grounds I didn't want that shut off either. So I began to write down each time I'd meet one of those persons what I thought I remembered about them and tried to form sort of a post-diary or a post-journal. I probably had about a hundred pages of this. I had a friend, a newspaper man, who said, "This is good, but it's formless." He said, "Why don't you try to pick out a character and pin it all on him?" Well, my instinct always is to think of other people. This is how I write and go about things. Our rule in the family was this: if we had a fight with a neighbor kid, if we came home with a bloody nose, pants torn, covered with water, or if the horse'd run away or something (we drove a horse to school and back), my mother's and father's reaction was it was probably your fault and not the neighbor's kid's fault. And they would never accuse or complain to someone else until they first found out that I wasn't guilty. "Are you sure, Frederick, you didn't start it?" So you see, I was trained to think of the other guy before I thought of myself and this is what happens often in my writing. I am not the autobiographical Tom Wolfe, who worries about his own navel and then starts exposing himself in his stuff. I was trained to think about the other guy very carefully, and then think about myself. So when it was suggested to me about my writing about the San, pinning it on someone else, the first one I thought of was Howard Anderson. I had been very sick at the time and I felt that if any-body was going to survive it would be Howard because he had this fight in him, whereas I lay passive. So I built it around him. Well, after twenty pages I ran out of Howard material and then I began to borrow heavily from my own experience. But you see, it isn't a true autobiography because the original image or impress is Howard Anderson. You know, though, my theory turned out to be wrong. Howard Anderson eventually died; I survived. His irrita-tion actually was an indication that his Lizard (the Old Man who runs us) knew he was going under. That's why he was irritable.

He was reacting against the defeat that was coming.

His sister was dying, and did die before he did. The whole family was wiped out except for his younger brother. Yet *Boy* probably does come closest to being autobiographical. . . . Ah . . . No one has read these things, but I have two new things that

I've written. One is called "The Man Who Looked Like the Prince of Wales." [1] I haven't decided yet to send it out. It's a short novel, fifty thousand words. And I have a short story of about twenty thousand called the "Apples of Paradise." Now in them a character has popped up named Alfred Alfredson who I've nicknamed Free. He is the truest Frederick Manfred. He probably will be my notion of my autobiographical image. I feel that I am old enough now to have a look at this guy, who lived, say, twenty years ago.

> *Will this be just a matter of essence though? Or fact by fact?*

Essence. The others (Thurs and Eric) are fact by fact. That isn't the real stuff, see.

> *I am wondering from the title "Prince of Wales" whether this takes place in Iowa.*

Yes, it does. It is based on the life of a cousin of mine, second cousin of mine, my mother's cousin who died. He looked an awful lot like the present Prince of Wales. There is a little legend in our family that on my mother's side our people do resemble the English Windsor family. Probably far back there they came from the same area in Germany. The English Windsor family came from Germany some ten generations ago. No, not that far . . . five or six generations back. And perhaps fifteen hundred years ago the same overlord was the father of many of . . . was the sire of both our peoples over there. One of his forms also happened to shoot down through my relatives and that is why my cousin Gerrit resembles the Prince of Wales. The pictures of the two are almost identical. And I have a boy named Free introduce the story. He knows this story and he starts telling it. And that is the first time I am really taking what I think is my essence. I am going to do more with him. Because I have never written about my family, my father's and my mother's families, except to have picked up a piece here and there, taken a shot at it here and there. There's a great lot of stories in those two families, and I will use Free as a device to get

[1] [Published by Trident Press (New York, 1965) ; reprinted in paperback by Pocket Books (New York, 1967) as *The Secret Place*.]

into all of them. That's a good name for him too, Free. Fits my spirit . . . Alfred comes from Free, not Free from Alfred.

> *You have obviously considered this problem from a critical point of view a little bit in the postscript to* The Giant, *this matter of the "rume," how you worked it out some years ago. Do you still like this distinction?*

Oh, yes. There is no doubt about it. Even though it's true that I haven't written a pure autobiographical novel, there is a difference between *Boy Almighty* and the *Wanderlust* and the rest. The moment you enter them there is a slightly uneasy quality about it. You're walking into a man's privacy. His kitchen. Or his whole life. There is that touch over it. I still feel that there is a big difference. Just go in to various writers' works. Go into Dickens' life. *Tale of Two Cities* and *Dombey and Son*, contrast them with *David Copperfield*. The moment you read *David Copperfield* you know that's autobiography. There is something about it that's different from the others. That's the rume, *Copperfield*. And the others are novels. And Thackeray — what's the one that has the name Dennis in it?[2] The autobiographical one? I forget the title now. But he has written an autobiographical novel too that the minute you begin reading it you know is autobiographical. While all the rest of his are historical or straight novel.

> *Where did the word "rume" come from? It's very much like the Icelandic "rune."*

Which not too many people know. Well, I wanted a word that would be new and that would mean something as opposed to the word "novel." The word "novel" is sort of a silly word. First of all the word "novel" is an intrusion in our own English language. A Latin word or possibly a French word. "Novel." It just means something "new." It's like saying "Midwest." What do you mean by "Midwest"? Where is "Midwest"? "Midwest" of what? The word "Midwest" is a silly word too. The "middle of west"? Well, there is no such thing. The word "novel"

[2] *Pendennis.* FFM

is the same sort of thing. However, we have it and we are stuck with it. And the word "fiction" too. Though there is something there because "fiction" goes back to a root of a sort from which it has been worked out. "Novel" just means "new." But I wanted something that was really rooted. . . . I ran across all sorts of things. I was thinking about cows chewing their cud twice so it's thoroughly digested. "Rumen." "Ruminative." In a sense that's what autobiographical material is. You relive it. First you swallow it. Then later on you bring it up and use it over again. Then you really give it to your body for use. Then too the word "rune" is part of it. Slash and stroke on wood and stones. That this is to be the record and memory of the fact that I was here. "Kilroy was here." Then one day I was looking in the *Oxford English Dictionary*, not on that subject but on something else, and in looking under "ru," going down the line, I ran across the word "rume." It was a misspelling of the word "room." I thought, "Say, that's pretty good. That's what my word should be." And I wrote it down. To me the word means . . . Etymologically it goes back to the Indo-European root "ru," meaning to utter, to make a cry of anguish, to call for help. Or a sort of singing, like a bullfrog might do in a pool. Just let his whole heart go. Rhuing either distress or joy. And of course that is what we all want to get into our novels. The best of either one, sorrow or joy, the highest at either end, that wide scope there. You take as your point of departure the private materials, things that have happened to you, and with these materials you build up an art form. When it is all done it really doesn't make any difference that it once came out of your life. You can have died and everything about you can have vanished, but it still would be art. The reader would know that it was a little "hotter," a little more intense, a little more subjective than the other one. But he still wouldn't have to know that it is autobiographical for it to work. It has to be as complete and work as well as a novel. In construction. Be put together as well. I might say, by the way, it's tougher to put a rume together than a novel. The main character you are dealing with is yourself, and you have certain leanings and bends. It's really tough to be objective about yourself. You can't always see yourself in the glass.

But the "rume" is more than being merely subjective?

Yes, it becomes objective.

It comes from the inside.

Whereas a novel deals with material that you see happen to other people. You relate it to your private experience. You see if it is true or false according to your private experience. But you still keep the original gestalt or construction from out there and build on the basis of that. You may even infuse your own material into the novel. In the rume and in the novel you start from different ends. But you arrive at finally the same thing. You want a good thing when you are done. Stand by itself. Whether you made it or not.

Has anyone picked up this term that you know of, the "rume"?

They've never used it. I have never seen it anywhere. Of course you know they didn't pick up the word "novel" for a long time either. Henry Fielding used it somewhere along the line in his essays. It took a long time, maybe a hundred years, before they began using it. The first novel really was written by Homer. And the next great one I think would be *Don Quixote* by Cervantes. Although he, of course, didn't know the word "novel" either. But Fielding formally set about to create a form. It was to be an epic in fiction, an epic in prose. Later on they called it "the novel." So, it will be some time before people will pick up the word "rume." Although I have talked to some people who tell me they agree with me and that there is no doubt that there is such a thing as "a rume." My publisher, Alan Swallow, has used it in several essays.[3] And Robert Bly, one of America's most interesting poets and critics, thinks it's a proper word and a good one.

Would you consider, then, one of your rumes, that is, either Boy Almighty *or part of the trilogy*

---

[3] Swallow explains the word "rume" in the blurb he wrote for *Wanderlust*, but otherwise I have not been able to find any mention of it in his essays. FFM

Wanderlust, to be one of your best books? Or would you now go to the other form to choose your best book? This is a nasty question at any time, but if the rume gives you perhaps the most anguish (as Faulkner has said about anguish) and perhaps might even be the biggest failure, would that make one of those books, then, the best one?

Well, my answer would be the answer of a parent. A parent would say, I love all of my children. In a sense, though, that is false, because if you were to probe into the parent by psychoanalysis you would discover that he did have a favorite. There has got to be a favorite. . . . I don't know whether I should answer that or not . . . I would say that as of the moment *Wanderlust* and *Morning Red* (which is a novel) were the two books where I tried to rise the highest and dove the deepest, but that formally, from a technical point of view, they are not as well done as, say, *Conquering Horse. Conquering Horse* does a lot of things that the others never got into. The feathers in that book are all in place. It flies. It almost flies too well. So that they don't recognize it as a book. It flies too well.

To take the two books, Wanderlust *and* Morning Red, *you identified them as two different kinds, one a rume and one a novel. Could you point exactly to where that difference occurs?*

Well, just from the physical basis, Thurs is a tall fellow and so am I. Though it's true he is an orphan and I had five brothers. But he is a tall fellow, he feels he's an outcast like I did. And I don't really mean to say now that I am pointing a finger at anybody when I say I am an outcast. I say that lovingly because the people who let you feel that you are an outcast may be right. Furthermore, as a writer you're right to feel you are an outcast. Because you have to sit on the outside to be able to describe what goes on in other lives. That's perfectly okay. This kind of points back to the problem of the rume. How are you going to be an outcast to your own life and be able to write about it? It's pretty tough to be a rumester.

Morning Red *sounds to many people just as —
to use the nasty word again — just as autobiographical.*

It isn't though.

Even though the characters are of a different size?

That's all different. That's some other people's
lives. Kurt Faber is a farm boy. He could be any one of a dozen I
knew as a boy who went off to college. And Jack Nagel, who is
a city boy, who is terribly troubled, he came from various sources,
two or three deep imprints, and much of it manufactured. I went
around looking at myself to see how I might have done what he
did had I been in the same spot. And I looked around at the lives
of other people. That book . . . I did a lot of dreaming about it.
And I often followed my dreams around. I would have a dream
about the book and the next day I would try to get it all in the book.
That's probably why it has that sort of "hot" context. It is almost
a living autobiography of somebody. But the reason for that is
that I dreamt about these people. I see them. I have seen most all
of my characters in dreams. I hear them talk. Now, when I start
doing that I know I am right on target. There are two people then.
It is true that dreams have overlays. There is a quality about
dreams that is hypnotic. And I want that effect. I want the readers
to think that they are actually looking at a piece of real raw flesh,
accidentally walking into somebody's bedroom. I want that. We
have too much of this other stuff. Sort of trivial. The truth is that
a thousand years from now, because of language difficulties and a
shift in taste as to customs, a taste for this instead of that, much of
what we put down today, and what you did for today, will be dead
to people. A book will survive if it has enough shockers in it. A
book to survive a thousand years has to be almost absolutely shocking to people today. The recognition of the shock value that is left
will be negotiable about a thousand years from now. Homer survived because he happened to hit on some "hot" things, which to
them probably were awful, but to us they seem only sort of covered
by a nice little patina of distance. And some of our responses to
him are learned. They aren't true to us.

These very things might make the book seem un-real now, as Morning Red *appeared to some re-viewers — the lady without the tongue under the Washington Avenue Bridge in Minneapolis, et cetera.*

Why, I've never met a lady without a tongue. I just thought that would be a fine thing to do. She's a foreigner, and so on, and can't talk in our society, so what do you do, you take her tongue out. . . . If I really were interested in surviving . . . I believe that everyone wants to put his mark down. If you are not going to be religious and don't believe in heaven, don't believe that you will have an eternal life in heaven, then your tendency will be to do something in this life that will have a touch of the eternal in it. So you try to write masterpieces. . . . I suppose if I were really interested in surviving I shouldn't be interested in having many sales. And in a sense I really don't get too disturbed about not having big sales — until my grocery bills climb to around six, seven hundred dollars. Then I begin to think that maybe I should go around stirring up a little following. But I am interested in finding out What Happened in What Is. Not in just the surface. The real stuff. And if this takes me occasionally into paths my mother would disapprove of, or my father or my grandfathers, or my uncles, or my wife, or my children, or even myself would disapprove of, I think I should still go ahead and take a good look at it and put it down.

This would be part of seeing everything in what we called before "the long view," instead of worrying about the moment. Don't you have moments occasionally when you would like to forget the long view and do something else?

No. It's fun to be always like this. I like to be wide awake. Being wide awake you've got all the doors open. You intend to go all the way . . .

*This dreaming, is it based upon some kind of day-
time experience that you have had? Or is this a
kind of dream that some people would call fantasy — pulling subject matter out of thin air?*

I think what happens is that I have become so
immersed in the problems of the book, and in the people in it, that
they infringe on or affect my conscious and unconscious mind both
about as deeply as a real living person does. Even my wife, my
children, or my brothers. Then after a while they become probably even more real in some instances. One of the first really
haunting ones that hit me . . . I've dreamed about all the characters in every one of my books . . . when I was doing the trilogy —
I had got into it a little ways in the overall plotting, I had written
maybe some ten, fifteen pages, testing this and that out — I woke
up one night. Oh, I'd say two or three in the morning. I was on
the margin of a dream and on the margin of a reality, that in-
between land there, when it seemed to me there was someone else
in our bedroom. So I raised up on my pillow a bit, wondering.
There had been some talk of a marauder in the community of
Bloomington. At that time there were very few people living out
there and they were quite concerned. Maybe that was part of the
reason. At any rate, I raised myself up on my pillow and stared
at this image in the bedroom against the wall at the foot of my bed.
I didn't know whether I wanted to wake up any more or slide back
into the dream. I was afraid that I would lose him either way. If
I rose into the conscious state too much, I would lose him, and if
I went back into the dream world, I would lose him. But what was
there was a real-looking fellow. Tall. Didn't quite look like me.
In fact, he was some different in the brows and hair. He had a
silverlock (which I put into the book then) and spoke a few words,
kind of abrupt. His motions and his movements and the way he
held himself is exactly as I thought of him as I wrote the book.
He was a real vision of somebody. Many writers have somebody
in mind, I understand, when they are writing a book, and I had in

mind this particular vision. While I was writing it some other odd things happened. One day, towards the end of the book in *The Giant* section of the *Wanderlust* trilogy, I was working out the next scene as I was taking a walk in the afternoon. I was walking home, and for a fleeting second I thought I saw Thurs walking towards me, coming down the road, probably because he walks down the road in the book. I had to blink my eyes. I thought: this is getting close to where a man is seeing hallucinations. I was so absorbed in the problems of my characters that these people were coming at me as visions. It is true that in my case I probably do see them a little too much at times as visions, so they . . . . We were talking about this earlier, about the characters' experiences in the book. It's so raw it's as if you are in someone's bedroom. I have had it already on a number of occasions . . . when I was reading about the Greeks, say, for a long time, and wondering what kind of life they lived, not just what you might read by Kitto or by this Edith Hamilton, or when you are reading the plays by Aeschylus, Sophocles, and Euripides, or when you are reading — who's the greatest historian of that time? Thucydides? You do get a kind of vision as you read these plays and histories and as you study Kitto — but you don't see them as you see yourself, or your neighbors when you go downtown. Real water running down the gutter, the exact shape of the sunshine on the side of a building, the true glitter of a leaf on a tree in a corner — that I had never seen from just reading the books. I think you get most of your information about the past as a sort of a book fragment. It comes through the prism of the book. It isn't quite the real stuff. But I have got so that I could force or push or lean myself toward wanting to find out what they really were like, that every now and then it has happened, for a fleeting second, that the curtain has parted. It isn't really a curtain either. It's a wall. It's . . . it's more of Athens than that. But for a fleeting second there I'd be in Athens. And I'd see the sandaled feet. And, of course, they had some animals, even see some of their own droppings in the street. And the marketplace where they brought in their onions and so on, I could smell the onions. I was there. It would last for maybe five or six seconds, then she'd shut off and it was gone. So, I was there and I will also occasionally have it if I read a powerful writer. Not as real as this, but almost.

I have had it when I am writing that I am actually there. I am lost. I have bawled over the typewriter . . . you know . . . when I was typing it up (I write longhand usually). But I have had it that when I was worked up I would find myself in tears, or whatever, or laughing hilariously as I would go along, behaving a little like a maniac.

> *Did these so-called dreams begin later in your career? Or did they actually start as far back as your first novel?*

They did. But they were vague ones then. They were fragments, et cetera. But I didn't really train myself. (I shouldn't say, "train myself" — that's bad.) The experience of writing the books gradually got into me so that I would have these dreams better and better.

> *This is like a stimulation of the imagination, in other words.*

Yes, and you get to be an expert at it. An expert writer. You know how to dream with yourself. You know how to use that side of yourself that is for the fantasies. You become a true expert.

> *How often did a dream, as it were, help you choose the subject matter of a book? Did you have visions about things that you thought you should then write about?*

Yes, the new one which isn't out yet.[1] I had an idea what I was going to do with it, generally. I wanted to do something about the Sioux uprising in Minnesota, a piece of our history that had vanished because the Civil War was afoot at the time. The Civil War was so huge that even this great Indian uprising, which was the biggest in American history, has found little or no place in our histories. I had that pretty well worked out. But one day I came upon a letter General Sibley wrote to his wife in which he refers in scathing tones to a young lady they both

[1] [*Scarlet Plume* (New York: Trident Press, 1964); reprinted in paperback by New American Library (New York, 1973).]

knew who preferred to go with her Indian lover into the wilds rather than go back to her husband and child who were waiting for her. This caught my eye. I wanted to know about that and so I read some more in the area. And I did finally dream on several occasions of a white girl with an Indian. Some of them were kind of along the nightmare side.

> *Some of that thought would be based on histori-cal reading that you had done?*

Yes, and then from childhood hearing about the Indians, which would imprint heavily upon me. I might say that my first impression of Indians were, as a little boy, seeing them coming down the road in their little wagons from Flandreau, going across the river here to Niobrara. They would occasionally come through where we lived and I was warned as a boy to be careful. That they would kidnap children. I understand now why they did it. If they lost a child, they wanted to replace it. They would do anything just to replace that child. Like you do with a cow that's lost its little calf. Or a dog that has lost its little puppy. The mother wails and moans until she has her replacement. The Indians felt that this mother that was crying should have a child no matter what. That is the reason for this legend. So we had to be careful. I saw them quite a few times on the road, so that would help lend plausibility to the dreams. . . . I kind of like my dreamer and I like to examine dreams. When I have a good dream and wake up in the night I try not to go to sleep right away, but will lie awake in bed and try to figure it all out. I read Freud's *Interpretation of Dreams* carefully to see how he went about it. I disagree with two thirds of what he says about it. I do think he did some tremendous things to start off some wonderful chains of thought, made some great inventions. But I think he gets everything backwards. About a hundred years from now I think we will discover that Freud has been pointing in the wrong direction . . . or pointing in the right direction, but from the wrong time scale. He is looking down at it from here, looking backwards. He is seeing everything through today's prejudices. Even though he is a scientific man he is still looking through today's scientific prejudices backwards. When the real way to look at all these problems in psychology, which they are "working up," is to look at them from the worm's point of view. Or, let us say, from our ancestor the squirrel's or from the baboon's or from the early primate's point of view.

> *Something like Vardis Fisher begins with in his* Testament of Man *series.*

Yes, very much so. A fellow in Africa by the name of Eugène Marais, who lived with the baboons quite a few years, just before he died said he was going to write a book to show that Freud was wrong.[2] Generally right, but specifically and actually wrong. Our civilization, and all the other levels of nations we have gone through, and all the things we've learned to do by reason and because of common sense, has gradually wiped out our most powerful ally. And that is our primate nature. What I call the Old Lizard. Or the Old Leviathan.

> *Just like the subconscious.*

The subconscious . . . yes. Well, it would be stronger than that. The subconscious is a piece of the Lizard. The Lizard is really the primate who is the wisest.

> *Old Adam?*

Old Adam, well, that's what the religious people would say. But that old hairy fellow knows things like that. Intuitively. Swiftly. He also, if you can get him on your side, will help you write your best books. Also give you the right response to a person in life and the right response to a character. Your childhood reactions to, say, your relatives. Why you didn't like so-and-so and why you did like so-and-so. And probably a more accurate recorder of what is going on around you than your today's reasoning mind might be with all that overburden of psychoanalysis and all that whole knowledge. Because the Old Adam is still alive in that child.

> *This is partly just insight, is it not?*

Well, it is the primate, though. The Old Primate who did things for profound reasons. He got where he did after

[2] Marais did write the book, a first draft, and it is called *The Soul of the Ape* [New York: Atheneum, 1969]. FFM

millions of years because he followed certain basic rules that were inside of himself. They were locked in. Say like a bird's instinct to fly from the north to the south and back again. If it became a reasoning person, it couldn't fly from the north and back.

> *This is more, then, like Carl Jung's "collective unconscious." Certain things that are built into us. We call them instinctive, but they have somehow always been there.*

We are erasing them. Except that they will still really be there, and will occasionally trip us up and cause us to do unreasoning things like, say, murder our brother or our wife, or kill our father or our mother. And people will say, "Why did he do that? He was raised as a good Christian." (Or raised as a good atheist.) But why did he do it? Well, the real truth is that in him the Old Primate, who knew that something was terribly wrong, that his mother was smothering him or something, said "Strike!" And the Old Primate is right. And she, of course, is wrong. The Old Primate still hangs around in us. If you can get him on your side as a writer you have got it.

> *Have you discovered, then, that this tendency to dream or to tap the subconscious, whatever it is, that this has come better in recent years? I recall that* The Golden Bowl, *the first novel, you said you rewrote it six or seven times.*

Seven times actually. I had started that the first time . . . . The first draft is the closest to the seventh, by the way. Without knowing it I went back to the first. Yes, I would say that. In the beginning . . . you know, to get that first book out, that's tough. It's just like the first piece of music you write, or the first painting you make, or the first baseball game you pitch, that's the tough one. To overcome that hurdle. To learn who you are. What your voice is. I was fortunate in my case. I tried to write a novel in college, got about eighty pages and quit. A guy who read it said girls didn't wear seven petticoats, that I didn't know anything about the girls. Well, I had no sister so I quit right there and decided that I didn't know enough. But the year that I hitchhiked across the country, or hitchhiked from my hometown of Doon to Yellowstone and back in 1934, I had some interesting experiences on that trip which I never forgot. And I tried to write some of it down. I had always wanted to write about the Dust Bowl. I tried various ways of getting at it. I read Steinbeck's *Of Mice and Men*, and of course was some over-influenced for a while. Then I read some Hemingway and tried to write like he did. But that was weak. You see, I had one good experience in that . . . . In college, when I flunked my first semester English, I didn't realize at the time that what was going on was that I spoke the American language which all along I thought was English. And my English teacher didn't recognize the American language and wanted me to speak like she did. Miss Timmer. So in second semester English, which was on a trial basis, I decided that the way to pass her class was to listen to her carefully for an hour, how she phrased everything, how she spoke (I was somewhat of a mimic), and then after she'd given us the next assignment I'd run from her classroom to my room with the echoes of her speech patterns still in my head and by imitating them write my theme or essay, and then I'd get a passing mark. In other words, I was just being a monkey. Aping it and giving it back to her. That was one of the reasons I thought that if I were to ape Hemingway or Steinbeck or some of these other fellows (I knew if I aped Wolfe that would be disastrous) that this would work out, but of course it was always weak. I was a newspaperman then (this was in 1937), and I had run across a rather nice friend named Jim who'd also had ambitions to write. He had written one novel, *Just Plain Larnin'* . . . . He had a party one Saturday night, late. It was one o'clock a.m. Sunday morning when I got done. Just out of curiosity I drove by his house, and sure enough the party was still going strong, so I entered. It was calm in there. I mean, it was no drunken thing. They were all rather intelligent people from the University, from the State Capitol, and from the newspaper world, and they were having coffee and beers, et cetera, with a lot of wonderful little conversations going. Someone around one-thirty or so happened to ask me — he had heard me mention one day that I had hitchhiked across South Dakota in 'thirty-four — he asked me what it was like then. What did it look like? He had never seen it. And I started telling them about it. I'd noticed before that whenever I tried to tell a story, or tell a part from my past life, that I could hold them for maybe five minutes, that's all, and then they'd drift off to other things. I had been interrupted so often I'd always been discouraged and so didn't talk much. But this time they listened. And they listened for about a half hour. In some cases they were laughing; in some cases they were very intent, almost sad at what I was telling them. Then I went home around two-thirty. I couldn't go to sleep. I parked the car. I took a long walk over the Cedar Avenue Bridge over the Mississippi River thinking about all this and I said to myself, "You know, I held that crowd tonight. There was about twenty of them listening and I had the whole room turn toward me at the end. What I was doing was the right thing. Whatever it was, that was it." It was "the voice" I had to find. It was a certain pacing I had . . . my own breathing pace was in it. The way I chose the words, the vernacular that I employed, the emphasis that I made, the story line that I developed, that was in it, so I went right back upstairs and I wrote all night long as fast as I could, trying to recall more than a summary of what I'd said. It ran into some forty-fifty pages. I wrote all the way into Sunday. Then on Monday night when I came home from work I looked at it again. And I said, "This is it!" I'd found my voice. In a sense, this was my dreamer, my fantasy man, at work. Because often in memory I had gone over that trip. I had remembered certain things, and I had enjoyed this or that aspect of it, had lingered on this facet or something and had built it up. . . . There was a spinster named, of all things, named Miss Minerva Baxter in it who picked me up in Presho and . . . that was a funny story. She had just bought herself an Essex and she had never driven before. In Chicago. She wrote religious maxims for a religious calendar. I think it was Methodist. She decided to visit her brother in Boise, Idaho, and was having trouble driving. So she decided that she was going to pick up somebody and have him drive for her. I was the first likely prospect she saw that she was sure would behave himself. I was twenty-two then and she was about forty-five, I suppose. So she made the filling station man get my name and asked for some of my letters to make sure that I was who I said I was. I remember I had FREDERICK FEIKEMA sewn in small letters on my college

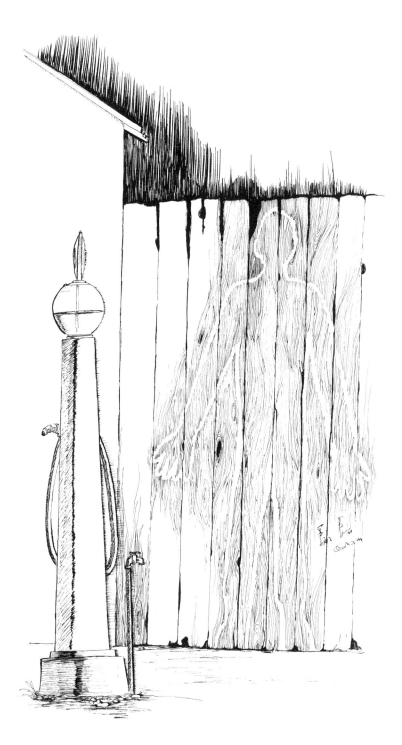

sweater. That was on the side here. She also made me line up against the wall there in the filling station and made him draw a map around me. She said, "In case something happens to me, you will know from this who did it." Well, we drove from town to town. She always said she was going to go only as far as the next town, you see. We hopped all across South Dakota. . . . I've built her up a little bit. But this was part of the dream-making, the fantasy-making, that's how I got *The Golden Bowl*. And everytime that I've gone astray, as I think I did in the first draft of the trilogy, it's because I haven't listened to my own pace, I have gone into how I thought some other guy would do it rather than into myself.

> *Now, does this include what we call theme? For example, toward the end of* The Golden Bowl *where you mention dinosaurs, the ancient beginnings, which are picked up again at the end of the trilogy . . .*

Oh, they weren't in that first draft.

That's what I wondered.

No, they were . . . they came in as I went into depth each time I tried. One of the versions was a play which was really pretty good. They were thinking of putting it on at the University of Minnesota Theatre. I had to rewrite the third act, but never did. I went into the novel instead. But as I went into it I began to dig into the history a little bit, of the time in the area. I wanted to root it in. One of the problems that I saw was that the people we know and from whom we draw our characters and our knowledges seemed to be two-dimensional. They had no past . . . not much of a past anyway . . . and I wanted to root everything down as deep as I could. So my first leap was way back into the dinosaur times. And then I became intrigued in it.

> *This would account, too, for the change from the farm novels, or those set in South Dakota and Iowa, to the Buckskin Man series. Is that right?*

Yes yes. It is. And also one of the reasons why I was interested in dinosaurs, too, is that in college every once in a while they called me "Dinny" or "Dinosaur." So I felt kind of sorry for them. So I checked up on the dinosaurs and the saurians generally.

> *How far is this Buckskin Man series going to go now? Are you coming back to contemporary subjects as in* Morning Red, *or . . .*

Oh yes. The new one that I haven't sent out yet, that I have at home, "The Man Who Looked Like the Prince of Wales," that's set about thirty years ago. When I finish . . . . You see, I have three Buckskins published. Then *Scarlet Plume*, which is coming out this fall, that's four. Then there will be one more in that set.[3] They will run roughly from eighteen hundred to nineteen hundred. I might just someday do a lumberjack, a Paul Bunyan, thing. I have been intrigued by Paul Bunyan. The legends that have been built up around him I think are a little off. But there is something sitting in the middle of all that that's very good, catches our imagination much like Ajax, Ulysses, and the great heroes of the Greeks do. He has that air about him. A real hero. But that I don't believe belongs in the Buckskin series. That's separate.

> *Does that suggest one reason for the Buckskin series? Or are you going back into the nineteenth century simply to find heroes that were heroic?*

Yes, probably I am.

> *Can we find any in contemporary society?*

You are asking the question, can we write epics in our society? I think we can. You see, there weren't very many heroes in Greek land either. You had to scratch around to find them. Ulysses was the big one, and then Ajax and Hercules, and so on. Maybe in all twenty-four major characters that the playwrights of that time worked on, and it took them some fifteen hundred years of history to find them. They had to scan back and forth for the twenty or so main heroes. We've only existed two or three hundred years. Actually some of us only a hundred out

---

[3] [*King of Spades* (New York: Trident Press, 1966) ; reprinted in paperback by New American Library (New York, 1973).]

here. Give us another couple of hundred years and we'll find all kinds of heroes. Even of the present day there will be some hero. Up-to-date, too. There are plenty of heroes in our past and I think we will find some in our contemporary society too. Things that have been done in a certain daring sense. Lindbergh is a remarkable hero, flying alone. A kind of an outcast in his own way.

Will we be inventing heroes too? We are not sure, you know, how many of the old Greek heroes had any kind of existence except imaginatively.

There was a core of truth there, though. For example, who was it, Schliemann, the guy that found Troy, the boy that dreamed that he would someday dig up Troy and then went over and found it, he generally proved the existence of the Greek heroes. He identified the wrong layers, though. But generally there is a layer of truth behind all heroes. There was a guy like that in the past somewhere. But there is one problem. Our old heroes we got by word of mouth. Transmission by word of mouth, that does something to them. They're built up. There were no pictures taken of them, generally. Davy Crockett, I guess, of him there is one. None of Hugh Glass, who is the greatest of all of our heroes. None of Daniel Boone that I can recall. We have paintings of him, but they are all imaginary. Of George Washington there is a painting. Not really a true picture though. Whereas today we are taking pictures of everything. We have all of these intimate camera shots of everybody. Of TV looking at everybody's life. And we have radio programs. And we have photographers and newspapermen. Something happens somewhere and everyone is in on it. They destroy the story right there by giving it too much attention. . . . So the new hero will have to be somebody who doesn't call too much attention to himself for a while . . .

I suppose the question you are most obviously interested in is, How does Maury come about? Where did he come from?

Many readers of The Golden Bowl *just assume that, because you made this hitchhiking trip, Maury is Fred.*

Yes. No, Maury is not Fred. Maury . . . Maury came about somewhat as follows. In 1934, in August, that was the year of what they call the Black Blizzard when there were terrible dust storms, and when we were in the depth of the depression and the depth of the drought. I helped my father get in the little grain that we had and it wasn't very much. It was rather dry. There wasn't much more to do. I was just out of college that summer. I thought, well, before I look around for a job, one of the things I must do is see more of my country. I had never been to New York and the West Coast. All that I had seen was Minnesota, South Dakota (a piece of South Dakota, Sioux Falls), Iowa, Illinois, Indiana and Michigan. Back and forth from home to college. But before I went — this is interesting — I was more interested in seeing the mountains, the Black Hills and Yellowstone National Park, than I was to see New York. I wanted to see both, but my first choice was to go West. So one morning I asked my dad if he wouldn't take me downtown to Doon. Which he did. And I caught a ride with a trucker to Sioux Falls. I got out on the highway, Highway 16, walked across town. I caught a ride with another trucker, a stranger. The truck was filled with people. I won't say they were bums or hobos but they were dispossessed people. People who had lost their farms and were going across the country. They wanted to go West. They had tried the East, and they couldn't make it. So they were going back to the western part of South Dakota and to Wyoming and further if they could. The truck was dung-spattered because on the way east the trucker had hauled cattle out of western South Dakota into eastern Iowa so the cattle could have grass in the pastures in eastern Iowa. They called that usufruct. The man in Iowa buys the cattle for whatever weight they are, and whatever they gain he gets that as his profit. I thought it was real odd that the truck that hauled cattle to the east to market on the way west should haul people. And I was one of those. On this truck was a young couple named Rivers, just married, from New York. They had never seen this country either and they looked at it with their odd eyes. They helped me see the country as I had never seen it before. Somewhere near Mitchell a young boy got aboard at a truck stop, tall, somewhat slim, and right away you could tell he was somewhat of a cynic. Not really a cynic, but he was embittered or saddened by life. We got to be pretty good friends. When the truck stopped, I think it was at Reliance or Kennebec — one of those places just before you get to Presho — it was nightfall — the young couple went their way. They had money for a room. I didn't have. I had eight, no, eleven bucks, tucked in the bottom of my shoe. I came home with eight, that's the way it was. I spent three on this whole trip. We had to buy water on a couple of occasions. Water had to be brought in, it was so dry there. This young boy and I found ourselves alone. He said, "I know a way we can get to the Black Hills." "How so?" "We'll sleep out on the prairie on the other side of the railroad tracks, because when they get to Chamberlain they lock up one side of the train, because all the towns and depots are on the same side. So they have a blind side all the way in. When the train stops we can hop out of the darkness and sit on those steps and ride all the way in. Ride in class." That was agreeable with me. He thought there was a train coming through there about four o'clock in the morning. So we went to sleep on the prairie grass. I had a little blanket with me which I covered myself with. I forget what he slept under. Just probably the sky. In the morning he gave me a kick to wake me up, and said it was time to get up. He'd heard the train hooting. But . . . I couldn't get up because by this time I had discovered I had a rattler in bed with me. I didn't know anything about rattlers. I had seen garter snakes and blue snakes, a few of those on the farm, but I was deadly afraid of the rattler. So I decided I was just going to lay there. I wasn't even going to talk to him. I didn't answer him. I didn't dare to for fear it would strike me. The rattler would strike me and probably the hobo too, for that matter. At any rate this fellow, after looking at me some-what cynically, finally saw the rattler and sort of hummed and thought I was foolish for not pushing it away or something, and then walked off and caught the train and disappeared. I waited until the sun got up and the rattler crawled away by himself. Then I got up. I found out later on, though, that when a rattler is cold and not coiled up, but lies intwined as he does when he sleeps, he couldn't have struck me. And if he could, it wouldn't have been very deep. Just the same I played it safe.[1]

> *That was all you saw of that young man?*

That was all I saw of him. And that was Maury. That became Maury Grant. Where did I get the name? Well, at that time I wasn't as conscious of names as I am now. I go about the name business pretty carefully now. I think it was Balzac who said that he could always tell a good writer by the aptness of the names of his characters. So I go about the business carefully. It is interesting that I should pick a name beginning with the letter M. Maury. They will tell you that generally speaking villains have names starting with B or P — that stands for pa, dad, bah. Little baby says, bah, bah. "Bad, bad. This is bad for you." A baby will then spit it out of his mouth. Those are the B and P names. Whereas if he likes something it is M or N or Ma–ma. For breast. It is interesting that I should choose Maury as the name of a hero. It has a nice M quality but it also has a hairy quality in the "aury" part. Grant is a hard solid good American name. I had a friend named Bob Grant who wound up in my other books later under another name. But at that time I just chose him out of thin air. Maury Grant.

> *A little later, in the trilogy . . . a number of people mentioned before it was rewritten, that names like Black Jack Hammer, et cetera, that these were a little overdone. That these names almost carica-tured the people they represented.*

That's when I went too far in the name business. I got too concerned with it. I didn't allow the Lizard to pick them. I picked them up here. That's why I changed it.

[1] Later that day I ran into Miss Minerva Baxter and her Essex. FFM

Some of them stayed in the final Wanderlust *version, like Sabine the sculptress, the headhunter . . .*

The rape of the Sabines, only in reverse.

Yes.

There was a play on that.

But Prexy Cee came out, didn't he?

That was too obvious. Oh, many of them in that first writing . . . a lot of them vanished. What I did there, I went too far into ancient Frisian names. I took old ancient Frisian names. I wanted to give *The Primitive* a denominational college flavor, but I went too far. In the final version I have changed all that so that the names fit the American scene.

One of my favorite characters — and his name is, I suppose, just typical — is Elof Lofbloom in The Chokecherry Tree. *Lofbloom.*

Yes.

He has the B in the last name, but he is still a very kindly character.

There is an M at the end though.

Does Elof come from anyone at all that you knew? Or is he supposed to be representative of the country bumpkin? This is the funniest of your books.

I had a lot of fun writing it too. I laughed all the way through that thing. It started out being a short story. Then another short story. Then I had five of them. Then I decided this is getting too big, so I backed up and rewrote those stories into a novel. That's why the first part is episodic. Until he starts taking that trip. Then it really starts to go. I'll tell you where Elof came from. That's an interesting story. I had in mind there a friend of mine named Edward who has . . . we were always trying to get Eddie dated. He had trouble asking girls. A nice fellow. We couldn't understand why the girls didn't go for him. So we were always trying to get him dated up. He is still a bachelor, runs a post office somewhere in New Jersey. Wonderful fellow. First-rate. He visited me one time in Iowa and enjoyed corn picking . . . no, corn shelling . . . and he couldn't get over how cows were milked. Every day he went into a rapture all day long about how farming went. So again I got a shot at this life. And I wondered many times what would have happened if he'd grown up in the Midwest. Had come out of the Midwest. Because I knew some who were like him and were Elofs. And then too I was having a little sardonic play with myself. Many of the things that happened to Elof happened to me in the summer of 1936. I was so broke . . . you see, I had been on the bum two years, as my dad says, out of college, and still I hadn't made anything of myself. I came home actually without a pair of shoes. In the book I have it that when Elof jumps out of the truck his shoes fall to pieces. Well, that summer I wore rubbers, outdoor barnyard rubbers, because we couldn't find shoes to fit me and I didn't have the money to buy them. I was that broke. I played quite a few games of diamond-ball that summer and I played them barefooted or in socks. So I took a lot of those things that had happened to me that summer and sardonically put it all into a small guy because I felt small all that summer long. It isn't really autobiographical, although I did take things that happened to me. Now the name came from this. We were living in the Twin Cities in 'forty-three or 'forty-four . . . 'forty-three. Our egg man came by. I never knew his name, he just came by. I mean, every week. We bought eggs from him every time he came by. He had big pink cheeks, nice farm boy, and occasionally I would see him carrying the *Time* magazine, et cetera. One day I said I didn't have the cash with me. We'd started a bank account, checking account, and I decided to give him a check. So I had to ask him for his name. I said, "What's the name?" And he said, "Oh, it's kind of a funny name." "What's the name?" "Well," he said,[2] "it's Elof Lofbloom." I was so taken with this name . . . . About two years before I wrote the book I heard one day through a neighbor lady that he'd died, so I felt free to use it after that. I knew nothing about him. The name came

[2] With a most wonderful grinning apologetic smile. FFM

from that. I thought it fit him. He was modest and carried *Time* around and was rather, I guess, a wonderful fellow, nice to his wife and kids.

> *What about Gert, then, in the same novel? I think of the lovely scene toward the end where I think they are almost literally throwing stove lids at each other, and flower pots.*

Well, I'd seen a few scenes like that out in the country. I've personally never thrown a stove lid at anybody, or anything of that nature. But I have seen a few scenes like that. Oh, I've seen a lot of Gerts around the countryside too. You know, large bosom, large strapping girls, that can milk a cow, can pitch hay, can drive a car, be a good mother, make fine meals. I used to . . . I still admire that type. I probably knew two or three. There was one that I really knew. I saw her on Saturday nights once in a while walking by. I used to think to myself, "When will the boys of Hull, Iowa, wake up and discover this beauty amongst them?" You know. I was too shy myself to go over and make a date with her. I played a little diamondball with her brothers once in a while. But I just saw her from a distance. She may have been the one that sort of set that off in my mind. But what I wanted for Elof was that she in a sense was a little larger than he was, sort of an earth, that she would be an earth mother to him, or mother earth, either way you want to take it.

> *To me, Elof in* The Chokecherry Tree *is not only more lovable but even more interesting than Pier Frixen in* This Is the Year. *But what do you think about those two in comparison? They are in the same economic and social condition, but they are two different people.*

Well, maybe you don't feel as warm to him. Perhaps I didn't feel as warm to him. Pier in many ways is my father and in many ways was one of my uncles. The farmer that won't listen, adjust to the American scene. He has all those old-country notions of how to do farming, straight lines, and hasn't learned the new things, soil conservation, and hasn't become really a part of the American country. It takes five hundred years to become . . . what is it? Eponymous? Autochthonous? Come out of the soil. Something that grows up out of the soil. There is a lot of my father in that book *This Is the Year.* The business of falling off of a windmill. And falling off of a barn. In kind of a grudging sort of way I show my admiration for him because I put him in a book and made a hero out of him. And I dedicated the book to him. My father was a remarkable fellow. I don't know whether this is the time to get into that or not, but later on I would like to say something about how fathers have more to do with making a good writer than mothers. I can tell you one thing, though, that got into one of the books and that caught my eye about my father.[3] I came home from high school one night. (I ran to high school and back one year, seven miles each way. Sometimes I walked.) I came home to find my father sitting by the kitchen stove which was his favorite place. His feet up on what we call the reservoir. That's the place where you have the water in back. That tank of water.

Cistern? Isn't that the same thing?

No, cistern is where we catch the rain water from the roof. This is a little rectangular tank that sits on the back of the stove and when the stove is always hot the water warms up. For teapots. When you quick want warm water you take it out of the reservoir. He always had his feet up on that. That's a warm place to put your feet. There is a nickel railing that goes around it and usually there is a coffeepot sitting there. It wasn't unusual to find him there. But this time he was holding his hand over his nose. And didn't have anything to say for a minute. My mother looked at him and said, "Yes, there sits your father. Crazy fool. Taking to jumping off windmills. And he won't go to a doctor. Who knows, he may be dead or dying." All Dad did was raise his hand off his nose a little and say, "You better do the chores tonight, son." And put his hand back over his nose. His nose was as big as a baked potato. Well, I went outdoors, and there my brothers who were home told me what had happened. I'll give you the picture. He had two more rows of corn to pick. The ground was frozen. He

[3] [*This Is the Year* (Garden City, N.Y.: Doubleday, 1947).]

saw that the windmill we had, which was an old-styler, a wooden one with a wooden fan or wooden mill up above, was turned wrong into the wind. It was turning backwards and binding and tying up. Which meant that he had to climb up to the top and turn it around to face the wind. He tied the horses up at the end of the field, crossed the fence, and climbed up this ladder to the top of the mill. And just as he got about into the platform part, as he grabbed the top wooden rung, the rung broke in his hands. Then he grabbed the next one. That broke. Later on he described this all to me. And that is why I admire my father so much. He knew what to do when it had to be done, as a typical pioneer had to do it. No monkey business worrying about rationality and is this the proper thing to do. Just do it, like a true animal. When you're chasing a mink across the river, the mink takes the right leaps and he makes it. Pa said, "I knew I was a gonner." He said, "I knew that if I fell straight down the angle of the windmill, the shape of it, I would fall onto the bottom part of those braces and supports and be all cut up. So," he said, "my only hope was to jump away from the mill. So," he said, "instead of grabbing for the third rung, which would probably have broke anyway, because by that time I was pulling at it from this angle, I deliberately jumped backwards as far as I could and gave myself a twist, and turned around in midair as I started to fall down." On the way down he knew that if he hit the ground straight or sideways or on his face or his back, he was dead. "So," he said, "I had to get some spring in me, like a grasshopper. I had to land like a grasshopper." So he slowly doubled himself up, made himself coil up so that when he hit he shot forward. I went out there that night. I found his heel marks about that deep in the frozen ground. The next thing I saw, about twenty feet ahead, was where his nose plowed through the grass. That's why he had this huge nose when I saw him. He didn't go to a doctor. He went out to the grove and cut off two willow twigs. He took the peeling off and put some homemade salve that he'd made of lard and liniment and rubbed this onto these two twigs and stuck them up his nose and then put a mold over his nose and this is the way he reconstructed his nose. He wasn't going to pay any doctor twenty or fifty or a hundred bucks to do this. Later on

I did it, which accounts for this little hump I have here. I had a chicken rack fall on my face once.

He begins to sound very much like Pier. Now what about Mr. Maynard? Maynard in the trilogy.

He originally was Menfrid in the old trilogy.

He is the father of Thurs, but he is a different kind of man altogether.

Well, in a certain sense perhaps I was looking for the father I thought I'd missed when I was young. Probably a false notion, because the guy, the father I had, was a great one. He was a hero. An old-style hero. When there was something to be done, he did it. Maynard was an intellectual type. I did miss, though, a father who read, who knew of intellectual concepts, who wasn't just passionate and direct, who was a man also of intellect and sensitivity, who could make fine distinctions, et cetera. My father didn't bother too much with that, except in work and in music. My father was quite musical. Well, Mr. Maynard . . . I don't know where he came from. He is literally . . . he is a figment of my imagination if ever there was one. I had a fine philosophy teacher in college, the only good teacher really I had there. A Dr. Jellema. But Mr. Maynard doesn't resemble Dr. Jellema. And Joseph Warren Beach, a poet, teacher and critic at the University of Minnesota. I always liked him in many ways, and Mr. Maynard does possibly resemble him just a little bit. I think that Mr. Maynard is somebody that I think maybe I'll grow to be. For my children. For my boy who hadn't arrived at that point yet, when I wrote the trilogy originally. The name of him in that first draft, Menfrid — I was intrigued with the translation of the name Feikema. I had stumbled across the Menfrid name before I learned that Feikema meant Manfred if you translated it. So when I rewrote the trilogy, I of course changed that. We didn't want to have Menfrid inside the book and Manfred on the outside. So we made it Mr. Maynard. I think in America we are looking for father symbols. Faulkner was busy doing it. Hemingway had a terrible father problem, and didn't lick it, and now has passed it on to his own children. Steinbeck is curiously silent about the fathers too. I think all societies wonder a little bit about the fathers. That is one of the themes I want to take up next in the new book I want to do.[4] I am going after that thing.

> *This may be because of the attention given to the family in Europe and then our impulse to break away from that.*

Yes.

> *We are ashamed of the fathers.*

Maybe we are. Maybe you're right. But all societies have overemphasized the son and mother problem. The father is there always so obviously in the scene that they seldom pay any attention to him. He is just somebody they can put their arm up against and say they don't want him. We have never gone around and looked at this peculiar problem. Because it is a problem to be a father. I think it is more of a problem to be a father, more difficult to be a good father, than to be a good mother. I think a woman can be a good mother no matter what happens to her. Even a woman who is born with addled genes can be a good mother if you make her. You know. (That's kind of a pun there.) But to become a father, that's something that is difficult to learn. It is very difficult to learn to become a father. Natural instinct and nature are against it. I remember as a boy seeing a boar going on a killing rampage. He killed over half a crop of pigs. Which is an instinct to get rid of them all. And in the horse world, look at what the old leading stallion does. He gets rid of all the males. All he wants is mares and little colts. He doesn't want any grown males around. And for a male to learn to be a loving father is the most difficult of all steps. A woman naturally loves her children because she carries them for nine months and then has to feed them for three or four more months closely and intimately. So that it is utterly natural for a woman to be a mother. She just can't help it. She *is* it. But to be a father, this is something you learn.

[4] [*King of Spades.*]

I have been trying to think of which women in your eleven novels would have been good mothers. Hero?

Yes. And Gertrude.

In her way.

Gertrude would have been a fine mother. Eva became an excellent mother. I have had some people complain to me. They say I don't give the women a fair shake. Well, that's because I didn't know much about them in the first place. I had no sisters and my mother died when I was seventeen. I had only an idealized notion of what a woman was like. I was raised with a father and five brothers. Of course now I am married and have two daughters and have had a mother-in-law stay with me for a long while, so I've got an overdose of the other side now. I come at it, though, from the adult or more mature time of my life ...

I think among the minor characters the two I remember best, or at least with most amusement, are women, and I am wondering where you got them. The two sisters in Chicago, Alviny and Alviry.

Yes. Well, I actually ran across them in South Minneapolis. That's pretty literal. I tell you, John, generally speaking, I make up most of mine. My people are invented from all over, and Lord knows how they happen to come together. Amongst the minor characters you will occasionally find one where I deliberately almost make a photograph. Dr. Abraham in *Boy Almighty* is the most literal of all. These two girls that you mentioned, these two old ladies, I ran into them in South Minneapolis. They had a little bit of a cottage all by themselves. Later on I saw something like it, not quite like it, in Chicago, so I put it down there. Mrs. Babbas and her troubles, you remember her? The motherly woman who took Thurs off the street in New Jersey? Her prototype lived near the University of Minnesota. . . . I will give the girls a fair shake as we go along, I think. And I have got them down fairly good. The girl Kirsten is pretty good in *The Golden Bowl*. And in *Boy Almighty* Mary is to me pretty good. At least I think so. Understand, I look at this from a man's point of view. I can't escape the fact that I have a strong masculine nature and was reared with mostly men around . . .

There would be some difficulty for a man to get into the mind of a woman and explain her as she is. Yes. And then in reference to your newest book, Scarlet Plume, *which has a woman as chief character . . .*

The so-called narrator.

Yes, why do that?

Robert Penn Warren used to be accused that his women weren't really women. Womanly. So he set out in *Band of*

Angels . . . I think it was that . . . wrote it from the woman's point of view. Did pretty good too.

> *Some writers do this just for an exercise, just to prove that they can do it.*

Yes. And then it also helps to give you another shot at the problem.

> *Yes.*

From the female point of view. I am always a little suspicious of that sort of thing. Believe me, before I decided that Judith should be the narrator I gave that a lot of thought. I spent a lot of time thinking, say, how my wife would write the book, or how my oldest daughter would write it. And of course the younger one. She is now fourteen. And how my mother would have written it. And then some of my women friends.

> *Did you also read captivity narratives such as Fanny Kelly's?*

Oh, yes. I read all sorts of those. There is one in New York . . . one happened in New York that is very famous too. Taken over by the Iroquois, I think she was. And then the Sioux Indians also kidnapped a white woman. There are a lot more of them. I decided that the way to get at the whole Indian problem, what the white man has done to the Indian . . . . Not only has the white man raped his land in many ways — I have shown this in *This Is the Year* — but in many ways the white man has also raped the Indian. He stole the land from the Indian and he debauched the Indian women and children. I thought one of the best ways to get at this problem was from a white woman's point of view, which would be the most touching, the most vibrant, and the most dynamic problem. Is it possible to see an Indian from a woman's point of view who has been kidnapped. This would bring the whole thing to light. I tried a number of little short sketches, one of which I sent to you. But then, when I finally did start off, I started right off with the morning of the attack and this allowed me some eighty to ninety pages of description and action. By this time I was acquainted with the ladies and could figure out prob-ably what they would be thinking. I think it comes off. I have had one person read it, a woman, and she made an interesting com-ment about it. She said "Officially the women will deny that this is the way they behave, but," she said, "actually this is what a woman would do." Then in theory, and I think also in knowledge — and when I use the word "knowledge" I say it in quotes — women are far more practical than men. When the chips are down the girls choose the right course for survival. Not the course, say, of intel-lectual truth, but the course of a living truth, survival truth. That's why they make the best shoppers. Are the best for detail work. And also the best to bargain for money when you go in for a job. Most men will tend to just go along with it . . . . This is going to be horrendous to hear. We admire businessmen in America in our profit-motivated economy. To me . . . I have often thought of the businessman as being the most feminine in our society. He is the one who knows how to make the sharp bargain. We admire busi-nessmen who make sharp bargains. So perhaps the businessmen are quite feminine. While the most masculine of all trades would be the arts. Because the masculine man tends to pursue ideas and pursue them in fields of art, as generals will pursue battle plans in the field of war, as writers will in the field of writing, as scientists will in the field of science. They will get hot on an idea and they will follow it through, no food, no sleep, night and day, even until they become emaciated. No woman would do that. And if she does, maybe she tends to be masculine, maybe she tends to be like Madame Curie and some of those.[1] But this was all in my mind as I wrote this. Final criteria always would be what I wrote. What would a high-spirited or hard-minded or real-estate–minded woman do in a pinch? Everytime I got in trouble I thought of that and then I went on. Worked rather well. Slowly, but rather well. In some ways I think it is the most moving, the most probing, of the books I have written so far. In fact, it is kind of eviscerative. When you are reading it you are going to be somewhat disemboweled.

Now, when you are preparing a book of this kind, do you spend more time trying to get inside the

[1] I meant to say Madame Sappho but Madame Curie slipped out instead. FFM

characters and understand their psychology, or do you spend more time on the historical aspects, since in this case there is a Sioux uprising and it can be read about in books?

Well, it began with the historical business. I checked all the records and read all these captivity stories and went into the Civil War . . . read quite a bit of Civil War stuff to get a feel of the time. About the bloomer girls — the feminine movement was just beginning at the time — a few women had begun to wear bloomers at that time. Which the men realized was a threat to them. But out of this reading grew some general knowledge, of course. Then I ran across this letter from General Sibley to his wife about this woman. That caught my mind. From that point on I began to drop the historical-looking and went more in for the character-looking.

Does this kind of thing happen frequently in your so-called historical novels, with Lord Grizzly, *or with* Riders of Judgment . . . *do you find a key ultimately that lets you drop a lot of other research material?*

Yes. Take *Lord Grizzly.* That came about mostly for two reasons. One, I thought that the characters in my books up to that point were somewhat two-dimensional. And I don't just mean the two dimensions that are out front — width and heighth. There was a background missing in all of them. The background point of departure was not in them. So, I became interested in the *Lord Grizzly* idea, the first of my so-called historicals, because I wanted to dig into our past history out here. And the other reason was that I was looking for material for *This Is the Year.* And looking in the *South Dakota Guide* I ran across this woodcut. It's of Hugh Glass wrestling with a bear — the knife, blood spilling — and this caught my eye. So I read the little inscription off to one side of it which told the story of Hugh Glass and it was sort of . . . . It was taken from Neihardt's book. I then started watching for stuff on Hugh Glass. I realized I didn't always understand what I was reading. So then I had to check the books describing the time,

Ruxton, Garrard, and . . . oh, who's the guy that wrote the two volumes, the famous set about the fur traders? . . . Chittenden . . . and that led to many others.[2]

> *Did you track down all the documents that were available?*

Oh yes. Another book on Hugh was published a year ago. Or last fall. It was amazing for me to discover that I had covered almost all but two or three sources, that I had dug 'em out on my own.

> *Was that the John Myers book?*[3]

That's right. I dug them all out except one or two.

> *How about capturing the physical location of the book, the work that you go through to make sure that you get the proper feel of the land?*

Well, now on that I have to tell you a couple of things. In Doon, Iowa, the Great Northern comes through town. There is a sandpit on the west side of the tracks. When I was a boy going to grade school there, grammar school, at noon after we had fed the horses we would go over to the tracks and look down into the sandpit and we would see hobos there. There was also a guy from Doon named Willemstein who liked to trap in the spring and in the fall, somewhere in Dakota. No one knew just where it was. But he would disappear for a while, then come back with his pelts and treat them and sell them. I used to see him around. He was a real old-time trapper and he had learned it from previous trappers who had learned it in turn from some trappers before that. So he would leap back into those Mountain Man times. He burned up in his little shack. He got stewed one night and burned up in his shack. About the time I began the book. Then the other thing I did . . . I had been through South Dakota again in 1949, but I thought that I had better revive my memory. So I drove over.

2 [Hiram Martin Chittenden, *The American Fur Trade of the Far West* (New York: F. P. Harper, 1902).]

3 [John Myers Myers, *Pirate, Pawnee, and Mountain Man; The Saga of Hugh Glass* (Boston: Little, Brown, 1963).]

First of all, I got a map of South Dakota on which every square mile was given. It was a railroad map on which you can check everything out. Every little knoll, every piece of brush, all railroad routes are all marked on this map. We (my wife and I) drove to Lemmon, South Dakota. We found the Hugh Glass monument, a little memorial, a piece of . . . I think it was marble . . . telling where they think Hugh wrestled the grizzly. From that point I walked much of the way mile for mile almost to Pierre. Across the country. My wife drove the old Ford. I'd give her the map and I'd say, "Now you be at this corner on the map and I'll be there at such and such a time. Just take your time. If I don't show up there in a day or two, you better call the sheriff. But just sit tight and don't worry." So I walked across the country. As I went along — I took little wax paper bags with me — and if I saw an interesting plant or something I would snip it off and put it in a bag. Or sometimes I dug up the plant, if I wanted to get the roots too. And sometimes I took ants. The ants are a little different out there. And some of the bugs. Took a few photographs as I walked along. A couple of times I lay down in the grass. Smelled the grass coming up around my face. I also climbed Thunder Butte. I climbed to the top of that and down again even though I didn't use this (the climbing) in the book. (I did use it later on for another book.[4]) But I wanted to get the feel of how it would look from Thunder Butte down to where Hugh was crawling along. Supposedly, anyway.

Was that west of McLaughlin, near the border?

Yes, uh huh, that's right. Then when I got home to Bloomington . . . . At that time I lived in Bloomington, on the bluffs overlooking the Minnesota River. We had bluffs which were similar to many of those in South Dakota. Long tall grass. Bluejoint. I made myself what I call a slape. That's something you can drag something on. A travois. A stoneboat kind of thing. I made this for my leg. Tied myself to it and then tried to crawl over this hillside to see how it would feel if I had a broken leg. See what I would do. In the process I would get tired and lie down in the grass. One time an ant was crawling over my lip, and I thought,

---

[4] [*Conquering Horse* (New York: McDowell, Obolensky, 1959); reprinted in paperback by New American Library (New York, 1973).]

"Say, I ought to have a taste of that too." How it was. Because he probably ate an ant or two too. So I bit into the ant. And, surprisingly, discovered it wasn't bad tasting. Actually, you know, I have quite a distaste for bugs of all kinds. But because this adventure was so interesting to me I had to know the truth. I was so absorbed in finding what I thought would be the truth of the day that at those moments I had no queasy feelings about checking out how a mouse or how a rattlesnake might taste. Any other time I would have hated it. You couldn't have got me to do it. But because this is a good job, and a job that I wanted to do, I did take these tastes. So I worked that all out before I began writing, physically, as much as I could. I always feel this way — I still go after the spirit of the book and the thrust of the book first, and the detail of it and the structure of it after. But in filling it all out you might as well have it true rather than false.

Right.

Get the material that's there. One of the wonderful charms of Homer is to read about the purple ribbons of the plowed fields, and the rosy fingers of dawn, and the color of the beaches. That makes it come to life. You are there. I always look around for the one vivid detail that will bring you right there. Like in the shocking grain scene in *The Chokecherry Tree.* I've shocked grain. You know, picking up the bundles and setting them up six in a bunch. I could have just given the motions. But I thought, "No, I've got to get the reader right there and a little detail will bring him there." I went back in my memory to the days when I was shocking, and I remembered one day as I was just finishing a shock and was just wiping the sweat off my nose, when a bumblebee came up and flew right in front of my eyes. It seemed like a century he hung there. I was afraid I was going to get stung by him. He flew first in front of this eye, then flew over to the other eye. So then I had the bumblebee confront Elof. And later on a wasp comes along. If I can get just one detail to do that, then I've got all the other details filled in. Yes.

After you have gathered the materials — however
you did that — what are your working habits? I

know that you had separate rooms in both places,
the shack in Bloomington and now the tower, as it
were, in Luverne. What kind of schedule do you
keep and how hard do you work yourself once you
get to the typewriter?

I am somewhat methodical, on the theory that it's all hard work. To get it done you have to work at it. It isn't just mood. Maybe a short story you can do in one blast, or one little painting you can do in one blast, but when you are writing a novel it's like a cross-country run. You have to brace yourself for the long haul. I get up usually at about six-thirty and make the breakfast and turn on the news and some music. I eat by myself usually and by the time I am done it is time for them (the children) to get up and go to school. I call them and then I go on my way. By seven-thirty I am at the desk. If I don't have it in my mind what to do next, I'll look over what I did the day before. Usually I find something wrong, and by the time I fix that up I'm ready to move forward into the new section. And the next thing you know it's eleven-thirty. I work by habit, as I say. Someone once asked Mr. Faulkner, did he write only when he was moved to write? Or did he write every day whether he felt like it or not? And he said he never wrote unless he was moved to write but that it happened he was moved every day. This is somewhat the way I am. Once I am engrossed in a story, the characters are all busy talking to me in my sleep. And when I wake up in the morning or when I am taking my walk, I actually can't get upstairs fast enough. I don't write too much a day, a page or two of longhand. I write until about eleven-thirty or twelve. Unless it is going very well. Toward the end of the book the stint becomes longer. It might become three or four pages. And sometimes . . . when I got to the end of *Riders of Judgment* I started doing eight or nine pages a day. I wrote the whole last fourth in a couple of weeks. I almost burned myself out doing it. But it wanted to come that fast, and the goal was within reach, and I was about to get across the river. Writing that first draft always reminds me of trying to swim across a river with a rope in your mouth. And once you're across you know how to get the rest of the bridge over.

Did this discipline come from being in the sanatorium for those two years?

Yes, that helped. I tended to be just a little bit . . . oh, I won't say dissolute . . . but careless. I didn't eat at the right times. I stayed up all night at times. For four years in college and two years after that I slept probably an average of three or four hours out of twenty-four. Because I had so many other things to do to catch up. I not only had to work my way through college, I also had my classes and my extracurricular activities. And I was an avid reader. I didn't have much time to sleep. So I borrowed some time from the future by not sleeping much. But the sanatorium taught me that I had better get some sleep. Also I learned in the sanatorium that big bodies need more rest than small bodies. This is true in nature. Elephants need more sleep than mice. And so on. This day-by-day regimen of the nurse coming in and waking you up, washing your face, brushing your teeth, the bedpan, and now it is reading time, and now the social worker is coming and . . . . However, there was also a reawakening of an experience I'd had earlier in life. And that was being a farm boy. On the farm you get up at four or five everyday and really become a morning worker. I think the best training in the world is to have been raised on the farm. Having been a farm boy is very handy for a writer. Because you learn early that the best part of the day is before noon. And there are other things about the farm that are interesting. In the winter you have a fallow period where you clean up things, you get the harness ready, you sharpen the disc (in the old days anyway), you buy a new fork if you need it, and you fatten the cattle. And you fatten yourself a little bit. Then comes the day of dreaming in February. Then in late March you get the seed ready. You fan the oats in a fanning mill. And you get the corn ready. And you disc up the land and prepare the bed and after a while you put the seed in. Then you cultivate it all summer long and in the fall you reap it. The process of writing works just about the same way. You spend a little time in research, or what I should say is everyday work, and after a while when looking that over you find some seed ideas that catch your eye, and you plant them in your imagination. I have often said that where my father, who to me is a great hero and without whom I probably would never have become a writer, was a farmer of soils, I am a farmer of brain cells. We use just about the same methods.

Both involve exploiting the creative process.

That's right. Exactly. Growing. Exploding. Knowing when to put in the seed and catch the explosion. In many ways I have done some of the same things that Dad has done. He often went to the banker in the spring. He didn't have the money and he would borrow money against the future. I have gone to the bank and borrowed money against the future. I have also borrowed money from my wife's mother on occasion as well as gotten advances from publishers when all I had to show was a synopsis for the next book.

When you have some debts, or don't feel well, does this sharpen your writing or discourage it?

I think it hurts it more than anything else. I have to also overcome that. The process of overcoming one thing is enough. Overcoming chaos in your mind.

Takes the energy before you get to writing.

It is enough of a problem to write. This business of living in a garret to become a good writer is just absolute bunk. I have strong reasons for saying that. It is not true. If someone were to hand me a million dollars a year I would hire me an accountant to handle the money, and then I would just sit and write. And I would write better books probably than I have so far. I am an old firehorse of a plug now. I have been trained to write and that's what I'll be.

With those novels which we might call personal, that are based on experience . . . the sport, Morning Red, *is the one novel that doesn't fit into any of these easy categories that we talked about.*

That actually in a way began as two books, you know. One was called "The Rape of Elizabeth" and the other was called "Mountain of Myrrh." One day, when they were still in a first draft stage, I was talking with a friend about them, Russell Roth, a wonderful fellow, good critic, wonderful friend, and he said, "You know, these two sound like they're alike; they have the same tone." And my wife agreed. Well, I sat down and thought about that for a while. And I finally decided, "Say, they're right." The thing that I was driving for was in both of them. Perhaps I could get it best out of them if I was to stick them both together. So I then threw everything away, made a brand new plot, sketched it all out, what I wanted to do, on some sheets of paper, and I went after it again. Now as for the people in it, Jack Nagel is the one that most people get disturbed by, you know, the one who kills his father and commits suicide and is guilty of the rape of Elizabeth. I had a friend named . . . well, maybe we better not mention his name. Wonderful fellow who came from a very fine family in Wisconsin. A very prominent family. They had an accident in the family and the family sort of broke up and this boy had trouble talking. He was very brilliant, and he had somewhat of a mother problem and a father problem. He had an older brother who was a favorite of the father because he was sort of horsey like the old man was, while this boy was sensitive and like his mother. The mother put protective arms around him. He happened to have an aunt who was a social worker and she saw that this was going to ruin the boy, so she plucked him out of that family and brought him over to the University of Minnesota. She knew me and she asked if he couldn't live with us for a while, with myself and my younger brother Floyd, just to learn how "normal" boys operate. We were young bachelors. I was twenty-five, twenty-six years old then. So he came over. At first I was afraid that he might be one of those slightly odd males, but as it turned out he wasn't that at all. He was just a blunted boy, blunted after what had happened to him, and he just needed some ordinary procedures around him. I got to know him fairly well and this fellow lived in Jack. There's quite a lot of him in there. A piece of him. Then the two times when I had operations on these hands it happened that on both occasions I was in the University of Minnesota hospital. As I was coming out of the ether on both occasions, I found I had roommates, both of whom couldn't talk. They'd fallen down on campus. They were GI's, going to school on the GI bill after the war, and they'd collapsed on the campus and were brought in. They had speech difficulties. I got acquainted with them just listening to their problems. One was married and the other wasn't. As they would slowly but surely unravel in front of me, I got a vision of what it felt like to be these fellows. I got to see what their problem was. It was very similar to the problem my friend from Wisconsin had. I said to myself, "Hey, here's a couple more of those personalities I don't know too much about. This is fascinating." And since I am a writer . . . you know, a writer is a little like a doctor. He never backs away from any fact. Even if he finds something that is utterly alien to his preconceptions, he still doesn't back away. He plunges forward. He gets to know things that probably the average human being shouldn't know about in the normal course of events. So it goes here. I went into some of these people. Some of them were aliens to me. It was interesting to find, though, that when I got to the far side of them, I saw that but for the grace of my father and my vigorous uncles, the males, I might have been just like those three fellows. So I caught a glimpse of that and made Jack Nagel up out of them. So then to counterbalance this fellow Jack Nagel, I used Kurt Faber to set up a different kind of male. The Kurt Fabers survive. But they are not as bright as the Jack Nagels. As man climbs up out of the primordial ooze, out of the slime . . . . I remember a line in *Morning Red*. The slimes of time.

Yes.

"My miserable worm's trail across the slimes of time." As man climbs up out of . . . you take the Christian who says man is by nature prone to sin and to do evil, or the evolutionist who says man is by nature prone to be an animal — they're both right. That is man's real nature. All the other business is whitewash. Intellectuality. There is just a little piece of the intellectual in man. A little bit of whitewash. And as he does climb toward that intellectuality — and it does seem that he wants to go toward that little streak of light up there — he runs into all sorts of horrible problems. He has to get rid of the natural instincts he has and replace them with something else. He begins by being one thing and then winds up being something else. And the turning and the pulling is just a little too much. The crest is too high. So he snaps. And I meant to show that snapping. Man will probably survive all right. Just as in this dream of Jack's where Doctor Decapitati . . . no . . . where a doctor[5] takes a cleaver and chops off the IQ's over 139. Anything over 140 is lopped off . . .

[5] Chief Decapitati. FFM

These first two paragraphs from the first novel going back to 1944, The Golden Bowl, *suggest something to me at least about the general theme that you are working with through many of your books. I would like to read them to refresh your memory and see what we have to say about them. These are in a sense, then, the first two published paragraphs that you wrote in your career. "Twisting its way among fat bluffs, the Highway reaches the Sioux River, crosses it, and enters eastern South Dakota. It turns sharply west on prairie farm land toward a cloud of treetops on the far horizon, which, lengthening, become towering cottonwoods. The steeples and smokestacks of a city come into view. The Highway hesitates beside red-and-yellow gas stations and oily hot dog stands. It enters the city, slips between gaudy super-markets housed behind the false fronts of old stores, runs beneath elms that spread leafy wings over high frame dwellings, and then sprints westward along a level plain." * The sprinting "westward along a level plain" suggests, at least to me, that in a sense this is what you are doing and right from the beginning.*

Yes, I suppose that's right. It was from a hitch-hiking trip that I made to the West, which I mentioned the other day, that started me writing "Seeing the Dust Bowl." You know, when you read that it sounded a little like it could be a modern version of *The Faerie Queene.*

It reads like poetry.

---

* Shortly after the book was published, I rewrote these two paragraphs and they have now been incorporated in the 1969 edition of *The Golden Bowl* [Vermillion S.D.: Dakota Press, Twenty-fifth Anniversary Edition, 1969]. FFM

Yes. Like the gentle knight pricking his way across the plain, by Spenser. I had never thought of it that way, but that's probably right. That opening section, by the way, has an interesting history. This book represents the seventh version of the same idea, and in every version the opening scene stayed about the same. I didn't change those much, the first four or five pages. It became this detailed because I used it as stage directions for the play version of the idea. The idea there was to help the director to put on the play, to set up the stage. You know, what it should look like, the road going off in the distance, the backdrop and so on, with Maury and the girl sitting along the roadside. The early version had a girl hitchhiking with him. Also a Negro hitch-hiker. The play version had them in particular. But eventually I tossed the extras out. Everytime I rewrote the book I did two things: I kept Maury and I kept the background. The other people changed. In the last version I thought of Kirsten's family. I forget where they came from. I have just a general memory of the originals for those people.

Did an editor insist upon this rewriting, or did you feel yourself that you had to do it?

Well, the first draft I wrote in 1937. This is the one I wrote after the newspaperman's party. After I had this one typed out, about sixty or seventy pages, I then opened up the scope a little and filled in dialogue. I sent that East without an agent. I think I had probably some five rejections on it. But one outfit . . . I think they were called Modern Age . . . they were the first paperbacks in this country . . . yes, called Modern Age Books, Incorporated, the editor there liked it very much. But he said the fashion nowdays is to have a revolutionary ending, and, he said, you should have a message in this thing. "Today the proletariat needs to have a voice and this book speaks for these homeless people, dispossessed people. Why don't you have sort of an uprising at the end?" Well, I wasn't in much of a mood for that. I did try to write one, but it wasn't very convincing and so I never put it in. Then I let this lay aside for a while. Instead I tackled another idea I had going, *This Is the Year*, which later on did become a book. The idea being that every spring the farmer says to himself, "This'll be the year I'll do 'er. Last year I lost my shirt and a few other things, but this year

I'll do 'er." I would do one draft of *This Is the Year* and send it out. When it had collected enough rejection slips, I'd put it aside and go back and do another version of *The Golden Bowl* and send that out some more. Then I'd pick up *This Is the Year* again. I did seven versions finally of *The Golden Bowl* and three of *This Is the Year*. Of the first two versions of *This Is the Year* I kept really only one piece. That was a thing in part published in *Esquire* called "Footsteps in the Alfalfa." I threw all the rest away. I burned them. But I didn't burn the versions of *The Golden Bowl*. I kept every one. I was curious about them, like it might be a first-born child. I was a little like a mother who tends to keep all the little mementos of the firstborn. When the second one comes along, and then the third one, she doesn't save all the diapers and safety pins and baby books, et cetera. She tends to forget to fill them into baby's daybook. But I thought it would be interesting to save this. I learned to write on this one. That was my teething book, so to speak.

> *In the first version of* The Golden Bowl, *did you concentrate mostly on the dust bowl incident without the broader implications that are in it now?*

I was hit by this experience while riding in the back of this truck through South Dakota. Plus the memory of that boy who to me seemed like he'd once been a very nice fellow, but who was now empty, hollow, defeated. I wasn't satisfied with that idea for myself because I personally wasn't defeated. That's why in this book I have Maury return home. That's the part that's invented.

> *You knew the other boy for just that one day?*

That's right. Just that one evening or night.

> *So that the actual discoveries that are made in the Black Hills and the Badlands are . . . these are more your own feeling?*

Oh yes, yes. . . . Oh, say . . . Standing up there . . . I know where I got . . . come to think of it, I know where I got Kirsten, Pa Thor, and Ma Thor. It just now comes to me. When I hitchhiked through Yellowstone and after I'd left this Miss Minerva Baxter standing beside Old Faithful . . . that's where I couldn't take her anymore . . . it was just getting too wild for me. She (Miss Baxter) tried to proselytize me into becoming a good Methodist. We fought over biblical texts all the way through Wyoming. I knew the Bible cold, you know. So everytime she would say something about "much reading is a weariness of the flesh," or something like that, I would always have a countering text, you know, all the way through, and that absolutely infuriated her. Then one night when we arrived in Ten Sleep, Wyoming, as we drove into town I heard a dance band in a dance hall. I said, "Oh, good. I can go over and see a dance. See real cowboys dance. And real cowgirls." She didn't say anything. We had dinner together. She paid for that because I drove all day through the Big Horns. Because in those days it took all day to go through them. She said, "I want to show you the cabin I got for you." The previous nights I took care of myself. I got into the cabin. She had the key and all of a sudden locked me in. She didn't want me to go to that dance. I waited a while and then I took the screen off in back. I crawled out and went to the dance anyway. I have a little scene there in *The Golden Bowl* about the dance. This sort of thing . . . .

Oh, a wild sort of thing happened in Yellowstone. I didn't put it in the book. It was too good. It would have pulled the book lopsided, way off balance. She found out that the regular wooden cabins there were too expensive. Next she found out that you could rent these tent cabins quite cheap. They have a wooden roof, but canvas sides and bottom. She couldn't afford two of them, so she got one for herself. She knew also that I was a voracious eater by this time. Because she was now paying for my food. She decided that she couldn't trust even smoked bacon in the car with me, so she took the smoked bacon with her in the tent. I slept in the car sitting upright. Sometime during the night there was an enormous scream. It was just horrendous. Everybody woke up, including the Yellowstone Park . . .

. . . Rangers.

We all tumbled out and checked what this was. And this is what happened. A bear had smelled the bacon. She had put the bacon between the mattress and the spring. While she was sound asleep she suddenly felt herself going up into the air, and she threw her arms out like this, and the first thing she felt was hair. She told me later on that she thought it was me. [Much laughter in the studio.] Then she let out an enormous shriek. Actually it was the bear going in there and getting the bacon. The bear heard the shriek and got scared. He kept hold of the bacon, though, and tore through the side of the tent and disappeared into the woods. Well, the rangers gave her quite a lecture on that, and then we all went back to our places, I sitting upright in the car and she back to the tent. Well, this went on and on. There was also a British family, a man taking in the sights with his wife and daughter, driving a Rolls Royce, with the driver on the other side, on the right side. That's right. They were sort of . . . the man was sort of a flushed Anglo-Saxon and his wife was sort of a lantern-jawed . . . typical lantern-jawed English woman . . . heavy chin and thin lips. Their girl was rather pretty. She kept wandering over to where I was standing to ask me about things because she'd decided that I was a college graduate since I was wearing a college sweater. She wanted to know about America. This the old couple didn't like. Though they didn't mind it too much because, after all, they were just out slumming in the daytime, in broad daylight. But my Minerva Baxter, she didn't like this at all, so I had enough of her by the time we got to the Old Faithful, and I parted with her there. . . . When I left Yellowstone, this . . . what I'm finally coming to now is where I got to Kirsten and her father and mother. I stopped at West Yellowstone. I had spent about a dollar-fifty of my own money and didn't want to spend any more. I heard the sheriff was in town. The sheriff represented two counties in that area. So I asked him if he had a bed for me. He said, "Sure, come on." He put me on a cot in his office in the jail. He said, "I'm going to have to lock you in." I said, "Oh, that's all right with me." So he locked me up. The next morning he woke me up and said, "I want you to come along with me." I didn't say anything. I picked up my suitcase and I walked with him through some brush across a lot and into his house. And there his wife had a great big stack of flapjacks ready for me. Lots of butter and syrup. Then he said, "Where you headed?" "I'm going up towards

Billings, Montana." "Well," he said, "I'll tell you what I'll do. I am going up the road about thirty miles and there I am going to take a turnoff. I'll drop you off there. That's a good place to get a ride." Well, he dropped me there around nine o'clock. And you know, I stood there all day. Not one car went by. It was beautiful. And wonderful. But I was getting nervous because I didn't get a ride. Then, just at dusk, a Chevrolet, a two-door Chevrolet, came along. You know, one of those little coupe types. A Chevrolet coupe sedan. They were towing another Chevy, an old touring car Chevy with the top down. In the old Chevy was an elderly man and woman and some camping equipment. That old Chevy had conked out. The front Chevy belonged to their daughter and her husband, their son-in-law. With the daughter and her husband was another young girl, her younger sister. The car was hot; that's why they had to stop. I got acquainted with them. The three in the coupe said, "A little more weight isn't going to hurt but we are full up in here. But you can sit up on the turtle." In the old days they called the back end of a coupe the turtle. So I sat up on the back, on that turtle, and I rode that way all the way up the Gallatin Valley, all the way up to about thirty or forty miles out. This girl kept looking back, the one that was sitting all to herself. She finally decided that she felt sorry for me, and she made them stop and told me to get inside. She sat on my lap the rest of the way. We barely got started again in the dark when we were sideswiped by a bunch of fellows who were in a dance band, somewhat drunk. They didn't hit the front car, but they did hit the back car. Broke the tow line and the old car shot into a ditch and the old couple went through the windshield and she broke her arm and he got all cut up. I was their one witness. That family stuck in my mind. The father, mother, and the girl. I am pretty sure that's where I got the old Thors. I just saw them briefly that time, but I'm just sure that's where they came out of. So, in a sense I did pick everything up (the actual discoveries) on that trip.

> *There are three high spots, as far as the theme goes, in the novel. When Maury goes down into the well . . .*

Yes.

. . . where he feels that he is reborn and makes it out again. And his then somewhat mystical experience in the Badlands. And the third one, I believe, is his discussion with the hobos, when he at last discovers that some kind of brotherhood is necessary. Now these three things obviously are put in by you. They are inventions.

Real inventions. Or inspirations. I don't think they were just inventions.

But these are the core of the book?

Yes.

As far as meaning goes?

Yes. I had that all in mind. I knew what I was doing there. Especially in that order. First, his being in the Badlands and the dinosaurs coming out of that. Then the somewhat . . . well, some of it goes up into Yellowstone, up in the Big Horns, et cetera. And then his sitting with the hobos, listening to them, and knowing that this is eventually what he is going to hit if he keeps on going. Which I saw in this boy that I met. I just saw nothing but sadness ahead for him. And if I had been one, I don't think I could have gone on. I at least was someday going to be writing this book . . . . Just before I wrote the book, I was visiting an uncle of mine in Iowa. They were digging a well on his farm. The guy, the well driller, had dropped his wrench dead center in the bottom of the well. Everytime they put the bit down, the bit would pick up the wrench and they couldn't dig. It looked like there was going to be water there too. They'd had trouble finding water. No one would go down in there to get the wrench. So I said, "I'll go down in there. It don't mean nothing." So I went down into the water and picked out the wrench and came back up. Later, when I got to thinking about this, I thought that this really ought to be recorded. That part is autobiographical.

When you use the word autobiographical, you mean something more profound.

Deeper than that. But this was something that I thought would work real well in *The Golden Bowl*. I had quite a problem at the end of that book. How was I going to end it? She is to have a baby and . . . But just how do you shape it off? Then it occurred to me one day that the opening of this book, this little poetic prologue, it ought to end that way. And I thought, another thing, this big cyclone system is moving over them, so why not have them — since this is not much of a wet weather country as the weather keeps sweeping by here — why not have the dead center of the cyclone sit over the house at the end of the book? Have them in the center of it? That gives a moment of pause and repose. They walk outdoors, and out of this a little poem comes up. This is what happened at the end. That poem suggests the future without saying that they are going to live happily ever after. It came to me just as I was going to send it to the publisher.

> *It's curious that Steinbeck in* The Grapes of Wrath, *which has many similarities to* The Golden Bowl, *obviously had a problem ending his novel.*

And he gave us that sort of shocker ending, which I never did think belonged in there.

> *No, and many people still complain about it.*

It isn't really . . . well, he probably got that from some Frenchman. Wasn't there some French writer who had a shock ending like that, with the same theme of a young girl breastfeeding an old man? I think it comes from . . . who's the guy that wrote so many short stories?

> *De Maupassant had many endings of that kind.*

Yes, I think he has an ending like that. He's the gentleman.

> *It seems, though, that what you did, instead of trying to put everything into one book, as Steinbeck did in that case, that while you were writing the poetry for* The Golden Bowl, *you were then putting, what shall we say, the details, the facts,*

into This Is the Year? *You have mentioned, for example, that you even collected weather data very carefully for that book.*

Yes. The first two drafts of *This Is the Year,* I tossed them all away except for . . . . Well, the first draft was a sort of series of episodes. I saved one episode and that became "Footsteps in the Alfalfa." The second draft was a very broad one. Had all sorts of themes going, the city, the country, and I tried safety-pinning the pieces together. The last line of one piece would be the beginning line of the next one. It was obvious that that wasn't very good. It was carpentry work rather than the real kind of finished woodwork that a real woodworker does. So I tossed it out, burned it, nine hundred pages of that one. I knew if that thing stayed around I would be tempted to try and fix it up, and there is no use fixing up a house that is begun badly. So then I got the idea for the new draft one day when . . . I forget just where I picked it up, but someone, somewhere, suggested to me that the record of the very weather itself was dramatic. The years keep varying back and forth. Well, I wrote to the Department of Meteorology in Des Moines for the records of the weather every day in Iowa for the period 1918 to 1936. I studied them carefully and I finally picked five years where the year was very dramatic according to the weather pattern. I thought, "Well, that's my ground . . . my ground plan. On top of that I will build my windmill, et cetera, and have my cottonwood trees grow, and have people stand." That forms sort of a woof of the book . . . no, the warp of the book. The woof will be the people. I had that one fairly well in mind by the time I started it.

Pier learned something more than Maury did. It may not be quite as important in some ways. It goes on beyond Maury's discovery.

Maury just comes back and is going to try and fight it out. Pier not only fights it out, he learns the lesson that you have to become a piece of the earth. Son of the earth. Not a destroyer of the earth. A son of the earth. Like a son loves his mother. You have to live with it and love it and protect it. And it takes the Old Dreamer . . . Incidentally, we were talking about the dream the other day? It's curious that I should use that word, Old Dreamer, in *This Is the Year.*

For Pederson, the county agent.

That was at work then already. And Teo, there are little bits of myself in that fellow, I suppose. Though I really had in mind my brother Floyd quite a lot. He had that sort of sterling way of looking at things all right. He was quite mechanically minded and yet was so in a poetic way. You know, Steinbeck somewhere in one of his books, I think it was in *Cannery Row,* talks about a young American who was an expert mechanic. Because he knows how to make love to his Ford but not to his girlfriend. Something like that. That the mechanics are sort of dull flat. The truth is, though, that a real mechanic . . . There are different degrees of mechanics. There are those dull-witted mechanics, but there are also those mechanics who are poets. And that's what I meant to show. Teo had a lot of poetry in him. Even though it was mechanics or agriculture he was interested in, there was a lot of poetry in that fellow. And truth.

I take it the name of Nertha, or Pier's wife, was not an accident.

No. Because somewhere in the process of reading Frisian history I ran into the fact that the Angles, the Angles particularly, and the Saxons too, had as one of their goddesses Nertha. Nerthus. The Frisians didn't have her that I know of. Just the Angles. And that caught my eye. She is the goddess of plenty, of cornucopia, and the way I use her in the book is sort of an irony. She didn't become the goddess of plenty because she was disturbed and hurt by the man. And of course . . .

Was that all her fault, now?
No.

Or do you suggest that Pier rapes his land by mistreating it and going against the county agent's directions, and does the same thing to his wife?

Yes, I meant those two, the earth and his wife. He does it to them at the same time. He isn't a lover of either one until it is almost too late. Of course, he at the end says his heart is still green, and he will pick up again somewhere else. As they all did, by the way.

It is hard to know what to think about Pier at the end because in some ways he has been somewhat of a villain.

Yes, he has.

We don't like what he has done, yet you suggest that he is a very heroic figure.

Well, let's take a look at the heroes of the Greeks. They're the same way, aren't they? By the time they come back, when they come back from Troy, they are all heroes. Yet every one of them has a disastrous ending. Except the sly one, Ulysses. And I am not sure that everything that Ulysses says he did was true either. Look at the horror he came plunging back to. He actually was guilty of desertion all those years. And some of the other ones . . . . I had somewhat . . . well, I won't say I had all those things in mind. But the Greeks had some influence on me. I had read all the Greeks by this time. Several times. What I meant by Pier is . . . actually, he is a hero. He survives. And the earth is still there too. And he can say at the end that he has learned some things and that he still has a green heart. He has lost one battle, but he is still alive. And you remember a tragic figure longer than you do a happy figure.

Oh, that's true. Are you beginning to suggest, as Faulkner did in his Nobel speech, that endurance is the most heroic thing we can do, at least in the twentieth century, or perhaps any time? Or that in fact this is the only thing that we have?

That's right.

If we don't endure, we do nothing.

The species that survived, they are here because they endured. And the human species if it doesn't have that same ability or capacity within itself for endurance won't survive either, in spite of all its intellectuality or its brilliance. The dreamers by themselves, the Old Dreamer by himself, he can go under too.

> *Then he and Nertha would be more tragic, though, in the long run, because they are defeated by people like Pier.*

You see, there is another side to that. I probably was pulled over a little bit by the usual story that the frontier women are supposed to have been so very unhappy. And I probably was one of those sons who thought that my mother was sort of lost on the prairies, you know, and should have been in the city where her abilities could have been more recognized and more valued than they were. Just as Beret in *Giants in the Earth* goes under in a somewhat similar way. The truth is, though, I was really in a sense wrong. Many women didn't go under. And they were noble women. I see them now in the streets of Luverne and Doon and all these little hamlets around here that I stop in. My own mother wasn't a Nertha at all. My own mother was the exact opposite. She went under because she had a heart disease. What's the one where you have growing pains? Rheumatic fever. And very bad, I guess. It's a miracle she lived as long as she did. She had a powerful body. She was almost six feet tall and strong. I remember one time when an old Fairbanks-Morse engine wouldn't start, a horse and a half, and she cranked it and cranked it, and finally, in her anger, picked up the engine and threw it over the fence into the yard where my dad worked. And let him fix it. Well, to me that hardly sounds like Nertha. [Laughter.]

> *That's true.*

She had in her longevity. She was valiant and yet was warm. Someday when this Free, this Alfred Alfredson I was telling you about, when he writes his story someday, why then I am going to set out after my own family, my mother and my dad, and I'll try to get them down as they really were. Or close to it. There will be some invention involved. . . . Oh, you have to try to put it down as it was even though it's impossible. So there will be some selection going on. And the moment you do that, art enters . . .

The Golden Bowl and This Is the Year *show the kind of relationship of man to land which has something to do with a healthy spiritual attitude. In* Boy Almighty *the relationship seems to be more of an inner one, of man trying to acquire physical health to start with and then of a very close spiritual health which has to accompany the physical recovery, from tuberculosis in this case. One of the interesting characters, who is perhaps the subconscious of the chief character, is the Whipper. Where does this concept come from and is this getting to be Freudian?*

Well, I suppose it would be somewhat Freudian. As indicated earlier, I read Freud. I think Freud was wrong on many points. Took the wrong attack. Went at it backwards. I wasn't thinking particularly of being Freudian. I was thinking mostly of setting up a background for Eric Frey and his father, and I wanted to have it that the few things he remembered about his father . . . . Well, there are two things. One that when he (his father) does visit him in the sanatorium, he's rather tender and kind to Eric, which I think, as time goes on, every son begins to see about his father. Sometimes Pa is strict with him, sometimes he is very harsh, and sometimes he is very tender. So to develop the harsh side I used a little incident that happened to me as a boy. I still don't remember quite why I did this, but I do remember that Aunt Kathryn used to take baths in the cobhouse in the summer. If the women hadn't been so secretive about all of this, that sort of hush-hush business ("Aunt Kathryn is going to take a bath, so you kids go play in the other end of the grove"), I wouldn't have bothered to look. But I did go over and take a look. There was this hole cut into the back of the cobhouse for the exhaust pipe of the washing machine engine. I got caught looking through it. And of course I got a real sound thrashing. So there is where the idea of the Whipper came in. You see, I extended that. I didn't want to load in too much detail on the boy's father. I decided it would be better to have an overall concept. Because life does have a Whipper in it. Pain.

> *Yes, and this is his attitude when he goes into the hospital. He is being whipped.*

Yes. Life has a lot of pleasant things in it, and joys, but it also has a lot of pains and this is one of the ways of expressing it, by way of the Whipper. I had nobody really in mind for that, though, just a spiritual concept. At that time in my life, as I recall it, it was just really beginning to soak in on me that the world is a rather lonely place in the interstellar spaces. There aren't too many other earths around where there are human beings on it. Maybe one or two. I was overwhelmed by the notion of the great vast spaces and distances around us. Just as the human being can be an orphan, the earth itself is an orphan. At first my thought was that perhaps the universe was chuckling ironically at our little ambitions, our little hopes, our aspirations. But the more I began to see about it, the more I began to see it was more than that; it was probably just indifferent to us all. Whatever we had we made ourselves, and we make the Whipper in our own image. In this case he (Eric Frey) made it the image of his father.

> *We are talking again about endurance. The will that a man must have simply to survive. Now, do the various characters to which you give rather interesting names — Calisto Sly, Satan Deeble, et cetera—do these people represent certain kinds of forces which are against us?*

Oh, I wouldn't say they are against us. I would just say they are forces we run into. Not against.

> *I didn't mean the will. These are things that must be overcome?*

Yes. Or belittled.

> *Do they represent any such things, or are they just characters?*

They are mostly characters to begin with. Well, they weren't exactly the way I found them. Calisto Sly — the idea for him came from a janitor who read a lot and didn't have any time for foolishness. They called him the haughty janitor. He wouldn't talk to anybody. But if he came by a bed where there were a lot of books, he would stop and talk and waste quite a lot of his time there just talking about the books. He was a well read man. When I dug into him a little bit, I discovered he'd studied to be a rabbi. But he rejected it and didn't want to take on any of its responsibilities with his kind of mind. Just that he wanted to taste and sip. He didn't even want the responsibility of marriage, so he took this job, did it, and then was free to read, and, as he said, taste and sip. I forget what his real name was. I understand that Calisto is actually a woman's name. I didn't know this at the time. Calista I would have known would be a woman's name. But . . . Calisto was also a woman's name. In history there is someone by that name, in another book, maybe by Eugène Sue. Edith Hamilton wrote of her too. I didn't know this. Satan Deeble. You see, the sanatorium is kind of a little world in itself. A microcosm in a macrocosm. Whatever is in the universe you will probably find in that sanatorium. Every aspect that you will find all around you in the world you will find in this little spot. It's all there. And I felt there had to be a Satan in the place. And there were a number of such fellows, there wasn't just one. A good friend of mine had a streak in him of always giving you legpulls, pulled off stunts, what we would call crude practical jokes. I saw some really fearful practical jokes in there. They tried to pull a couple on me, but I saw them coming. In one case I decided to let them go ahead with it; let them have a little fun. They were chronics. By a chronic we mean a man that is just sick enough to stay, and too sick to go out, but yet really not sick enough to keep in bed. These fellows were full of cruel pranks. There were a number of those and I combined them all into one and called them Satan Deeble. Satan Deeble takes Eric through the tunnels and shows him these cadavers and chopped-up lungs. It happened that I personally had found them alone. I went down there one day, went looking, and I found them there myself. But it occurred to me that this is what a practical joker might do some day. And also that last time when

I was rewriting the book I was beginning to invent and create. I thought that this is the kind of thing that a Satan Deeble would show them. Show them Dante's Hell.

I was going to say, it is just a symbolic relationship here.

Yes, purgatory. Showing what you have down in purgatory.

Now most of these minor characters are in one or another way escapists themselves.

Yessir.

So Eric had to fight them.

Or rather relate himself to them for survival. One interesting thing happened. I think I mentioned earlier that I quite deliberately tried to portray the doctor as he was. Dr. Abraham. The actual doctor's name was Sumner Cohen. He is still my doctor today. By the way, when I got through writing the book I had him read it carefully to check everything out. When he got all done, he said two things. He was quite curt about it. He said, one, he had never really known how a patient felt, he had never really seen this whole problem from the point of view of the patient — it was always from the doctor's. This time he saw it from the patient's. This would be very valuable to him. Two, everything was plausible in the book. Nothing was overdrawn or too realistic or raw or anything. Except that he thought the operation was atypical, where Fawkes loses his life. I said to him about the operation, "But it has happened." "Yes." "Well," I said, "sometimes a writer to make his point has to take an atypical case or an atypical scene to point something up." This Fawkes fellow was an interesting guy. I didn't know a fellow like that actually. I saw a man briefly who came to my room, in a bathrobe, and who asked me for a book I had. I think it was Darwin's *Origin of Species* that I was reading. He had sort of wimmering brown eyes, sympathetic yet piercing. We looked at each other maybe a minute or two, and then he went his way, except to say that he was going to have an operation the next day. Then I also saw him a little later. That same evening I was lying on my back seeing a movie. Those of us who were too sick to sit up could lay down on a litter and look at a movie sideways. As he walked by he pinched my toe. That's all the contact I had with Ted Struikens. About three or four years after the book was published the phone rings one night and a rather breathless woman says — I had met her at some party apparently — she says, "Fred, is Fawkes in *Boy Almighty* my brother Ted Struikens?" I never knew she had a brother. I said, "Well, I don't know. What do you mean?" She said, "Well, Fawkes is Ted to a T exactly. You've got his spirit, his whole essence, everything about him, just the way Ted was." I told her that I'd just met Ted Struikens for a few brief moments, but that I was struck by him because it was rather lonesome in that place. There weren't too many people who read. . . . I had a barber in my room for a while. And a farmer. And a filling station operator. And I had Howard Anderson the china shop man. Finally I wound up with two doctors. To turn the picture over the other way, another fellow I had as a roommate, Dr. Wilmer, has thought that he really was Fawkes, that I meant to picture him. Which is interesting to me because I never gave Wilmer a single thought, that part of it anyway, that he would be Fawkes. It is interesting to see that he should think that he was Fawkes. I mean, that he reads himself into that. That's always amusing.

Don't readers do this quite often?

Oh yes.

Even when they complain about being identified, they are really quite happy.

That you should happen to look in their direction. Fawkes to me — I got to love him and I liked him very much . . . . There was a love affair in my room that I didn't dare to go into in that book for fear it would pull it off base. I may someday make a play out of that. Huck . . . the man was Huck . . . I forget his last name. He'd met a beautiful blond girl and had fallen in love with her, and just at the time when they'd fallen in love and had kissed for the first time — a rather Christian purehearted kiss — they both got the word that they had tuberculosis. They wondered if they should run away and get married for at least a month. Then at least they would have had that. Because they thought they were doomed. But they didn't run away and marry. When I first moved into his room, he was writing a daily letter to her and getting one from her daily. After a while I became somewhat intrigued in this. But I didn't say much. Usually we didn't pry into each other's affairs. You were living so terribly intimate together as it was, it was a relief not to pry and not to know things. You got to know too many things. But eventually I found out about them, that they hadn't seen each other in some three or four months, and that they had been trying to arrange that they could go to the movie on the same night and then somehow have the ushers somehow put the two of them alone somewhere together. But it never quite worked out. Finally some of us other patients got interested in this problem and we did a little talking to the ushers and tried to arrange that they could meet alone. And then I knew the diet kitchen girl, who ran that a little bit. She and I used to fight over the diet. I complained that I didn't get enough greens and bloody meat. You know how I wanted that. I told her that all these carbohydrates I was getting weren't doing me any good, just making me fat and still not helping me out. What I wanted was greens and reds. She became intrigued in this wonderful love story and I suggested to her that she get in touch with the two ushers, one from the girl's side and one from the boy's side, and arrange for a tryst up in her diet kitchen. And this actually was arranged, and they were in the diet kitchen, and no one knows what happened there, and about a week later both died.[1] I always thought that would make a great story. But you see, to put that in that book would have made it lopsided, made it swell out in a direction that would spoil it. I had a little start of it in there in an early draft, but I cut it out. It was hard to do, but I had to cut it out. Absolutely. It would have ruined the book. And it's worked. It's a story in its own right. It was a curious thing, but every night when Huck was through reading her letter — he would read it three times — just as he went to bed he would burn it. The nurses always complained about the ashes they found in the ashtray by his bed. But he always burned

---

[1] Actually, Huck died several months later in another sanatorium. FFM

the letter. He could never save it.[2] I would have given anything to know what was in those letters.

> *By the time you got to the end of the book, you were concerned in some of the later scenes with Eric trying to find his direction. This is out by the railroad tracks near your Bloomington home.*

Yes. Near Oak Terrace, Minnesota.

> *Now, can this be blown up, let's say into a kind of symbol? In the relation to some of your other books, is the character trying to find his direction? Is this the most important thing that finally comes out of the book?*

Well, this is what happened to me. When I finally became ambulatory and could walk again . . . The goal of every patient there was to be allowed to take a walk outdoors, first fifteen minutes, then a half hour, and then an hour, and then two hours. I finally got to where I could be outdoors two hours. They always warned me that climbing a hill was rough. So I made up my mind that the day I could walk up a certain nearby hill without pausing, that would be the day I would be ready to go home. So I set that as my private goal. And I did finally make the hill one day, and kept on walking. And I had this wonderful experience walking over to the railroad trestle and seeing this train come by. There went life with all of its color and gay people going on trips somewhere, some far distance. This is what I wanted. So I thought, why not end the book on that? That points everything up. So I used it. When I was writing it I then became aware that there was something going on . . . I have a theory about that. You should never begin with a symbol. You should never begin with an idea, that is, an abstract idea. You should never begin with just a bald plot. You should always begin with blood and tissue and flesh and instinct and sensuality, and if something in you, the Old Lizard in you, wants to talk about that stuff, he knows there is a meaning behind it there which, if you will pursue it in your writing, by the

[2] Sometimes he would tear it to fine bits and put it in his waste container. FFM

time he gets to the end of the book that meaning will pop through. And then it means something. Only then does the symbol mean anything. Otherwise it is foolish to chase symbols. That is what is wrong with much modern writing today. The boys are taught in classrooms and colleges to pursue symbols. "This symbol is in *Heart of Darkness*," the profs say, "and this idea is in Faulkner's book," et cetera. So when the kids start writing a book they grab at it at the wrong end. They say, "Well, I have this idea here, I'm going to make this into a book." That's the way it doesn't work. That's exactly wrong. And this is what's wrong, by the way, with Freud. Freud begins his theories with an intellectual notion and finds evidence for it all through human society, when the truth of it is he should really begin from the worm's point of view and then look up to the other end and there see the relationships. Or from the baboon's point of view.

> *You would agree with William Carlos Williams that the writer starts with images or with things, and meaning develops later from these things.*

Even things and images is only half the way down the road. I would say that . . .

> *Well, take the images away and just say "things."*

Things, or happenings, things that have happened to you that you can't forget. Now, there is a reason why you can't forget them. You better pay attention to that. In the middle of them there will be something that you can pull up and abstract after you are done.

> *I am thinking, for example, in* The Chokecherry Tree, *how the chokecherry tree and the cottonwood tree . . .*

Yes.

> *. . . a large tree, a small tree . . . and Elof Lofbloom is the chokecherry tree. But who is the cottonwood? Thurs, later?*

You see, I was going to have that (the story in *The Chokecherry Tree*) as part of the trilogy at one time. That general notion. But it happened that I started writing a few short stories on this Elof, and then I decided, oh, heck, I think I'll just keep it by itself. Then it occurred to me that the two trees that I remembered most in my boyhood were the cottonwoods, which are tall and leafy, rather beautiful (I can't understand why the people don't like the cottonwood . . . they say they don't like the cotton flying all around . . . to me that's beautiful . . . that's the golden fleece) and then the chokecherry trees which I used to sample at the end of the field. It always left a tart taste in my mouth. And it always is short. And it's short-lived. And I thought, well, here is a big man and here is a little man. . . . That summer while I was writing the book *The Chokecherry Tree*, I felt a little like the chokecherry tree. I also had this taste in my mouth. So I then wrote the book. Almost out of the taste, I might say. It started out of the taste.

> *Is that why it becomes comic? This is the funniest of all your novels.*

Yeh, because there is a ride. . . . You see, a man who eats a couple of handfuls of chokecherries is going to look like he is just about to break out into a smile, kind of puckered up, you see. While the cottonwood tree just stands huge and stately. . . . There were also some other things going on in there. I have often been asked, by the way, why I have the recipe at the end of the book. Which, by the way, works. A lot of people have taken this recipe and made fine chokecherry jam out of it. I guess you told me about that.

> *Yes, this happened in Denver. A graduate student who had taken Western Literature from me gave the recipe to a customer at the library. She couldn't find it anywhere except in your book. But I never heard whether it worked for her.*

Well, I know that it works because it comes from Aunt Kathryn's recipe book, with all of her little comments practically intact. I wrote them right in. I did that for a reason. I wanted that book to end on a simple hard fact of domesticity. This is what he (Elof) settled for at the end. He isn't going to be the great man, be the hero as he thought. The original title of the book, by the way, was "Hero." Just "Hero," meant in irony.

Yes.

He was just going to be Elof married to Gert running a filling station next to a chokecherry tree from which you can make some very fine jam. The jam isn't tart; it has sort of a pecan taste, sort of. Best jelly in the world is chokecherry jelly. There's nothing like it.

Now, is this the sort of novel that you would write — pardon the expression — only as a younger man? Or do you ever feel like going back to that kind of broad comedy?

This new one I haven't sent out, "The Man Who Looked Like the Prince of Wales," has touches of that all through it. Lot of humor in that book. Very sad and very humorous both. And about the same length and the same kind of writing. . . . No, I have three or four . . . . If I can just live another forty years, I'll have about a half dozen like that.

Set in Iowa?

Not necessarily. But there will be more like that.

That brings up an interesting question. Are all of these humorous notions out of Iowa, out of the farm land?

No, because one of them that I was talking about with my wife the other day is set of all places in Macalester College. I mean, I got the idea out of Macalester College. No, this will be set in the city, in the attorney general's office in St. Paul. I happened to be telling my daughter and her friends about it and they were laughing for hours. So I knew that I had a good tale on my hands. I scribbled down some notes, I know it won't run more than about two hundred pages. I just have to live long enough and I'll get it in.

What about some of the other characters in The Chokecherry Tree, *like the young Domeny Hillich, and Fats or Fatso.*

Well, for domenys I used to have a slight antagonism going for them. I worked my way through college as a janitor. My dad gave me fifty bucks and that's all I got. I worked my way through college. It happened that I was a janitor at Calvin College, in the dormitory there, and a good share of the fellows, almost all of them on the top floor, and a good part of them on the second floor, were . . . what do you call them? . . . pre-seminarians. I had quite an edgy experience with those fellows. They were the smuggest bunch of boys I had ever known. They never took care of their lavatories, and their rooms were always a mess. I think they were raised by mothers who knew they were going to become ministers, and so were privileged characters and didn't have to pick up after themselves. I tried to stress in those days . . . I tell my kids that a true aristocrat always cleans up after himself. In the world of the cats, the cat that you think the most of, the big tomcat, is the one who is the neatest with his fur and hide. He cleans up after himself. That is the true aristocrat. The lion is the king of the animals and yet he is one of the cleanest animals on the earth. He takes care of himself. The she-lion doesn't take care of him. He takes care of himself. These fellows were a mess. But I have gotten over that, and I have now met some ministers that I like, and in one story later on I did portray a minister in a pretty nice way, I think. . . . Fats. There was a guy. He is also based somewhat on a fellow that I met one time who died of tuberculosis. The family that I got my tuberculosis from. Everyone in that family died of miliary tuberculosis. I am the only one who survived in that household. Fats was one of those.

This was near the University in Minneapolis?

No, it was in Sioux Falls here. He was a Sioux Falls boy. His name was something else. I made up this name of Fats. Pott, I think it was.[3] I was working at my dad's filling station in 'thirty-six in September. It had just been announced that I had

---

[3] Pott is also an invented name. FFM

won some kind of literary prize in Grand Rapids, Michigan. I got second prize. Peter DeVries got first, I got second, and David Cornel De Jong got third. The stories were to be printed in the Dutch Christian Reformed *Banner*, but when the editor discovered the judges had chosen us, he wouldn't print them. He gave us the money. They never were printed, but we got the money. I had that twenty-five bucks and I'd just bought my first new pair of shoes for that summer. I had been running around in rubbers. Fats comes by and he suggests that I go out and help him sell Jewel Tea, some product that you went with from house to house.

> *It was a truck that went around from place to place.*

And I went along and went to a couple of their conventions. But I was an utter flop. I could get into every household in the country. The women felt sorry for me the minute they saw me come in the door. This was a challenge to their cooking skills. They wanted to get some flesh on this empty frame. But when it came time for me to get them to sign a little receipt that they had received the free bowl from me, that I had made a sale, I couldn't quite do it. I just didn't have that pounce in me. That tiger. I still can't do that to people. I think that's an imposition. If they want it, fine, but you shouldn't shove it at them. So I used all this, gave it all to Elof. Meanwhile, Fats was having great success. He also could get into the house. He also looked hungry. But he could get the girls to sign. Sometimes he stayed longer than usual. He made a lot of seductions along the way. And would boast about them. He could see that I was relatively a naïve fellow, and he thought it was his duty to introduce me into the ways of a man of the world and tried very hard to get me, as he called it, "fixed up." That's why I had that hilarious scene about this big school teacher. The girl that bounced into the stove, et cetera. There was such a girl. In the book I have a rather large woman throwing little Elof around . . .

In any case, Lord Grizzly *is the book, whether you like it or not, that made you famous. It is the one you have the reputation for in most circles, isn't it?*

I don't know, John.

It's the one that sold the best — how about that?

Yes, and it is being printed again this year.

In this country?

And in England. So I guess after ten years its being reprinted again means something.

Did the fact that it sold well have anything to do with your decision to continue the Buckskin Man series?

No. I had that pretty well worked out by that time. I was going to explore that whole era from around 1800 and on. For this part of the country. That's when the white man hit it, more or less. Actually, the white man came here a little earlier than that, but they were only a few riverboat men . . . not riverboat men, but trappers. Early trappers and traders. No, I had that pretty well worked out in my mind, how I was going to go on with it. In a general way. I didn't have it specifically worked out. But I wanted to hit about every twenty-five or every twenty years or so from 1800 and on. I by this time had the concept, which had been vague before that, that I would like to get this all into fiction. The history of the white man and the history of this era from 1800 on until the day I died. A long mural. Or a hallway full of murals. The day I died it would be pretty well worked out. You take a tour around that hall and you'll know it. You see, it's my theory that if you want to know something about a time and place you don't go to historians particularly, necessarily, and you don't have to go to the law courts for the cases they have there, and to the newspapers, for the truth. If you really want to soak yourself up and find out

what happened in a given time, go to the novelist. The Victorian age, for example. Where do you get the best picture? Dickens, Thackeray, and . . . who was the guy that wrote *Moonstone*? . . . Collins. That is, by the way, a marvelous book. One book, and that's all they had from him.

> *Well, did you choose Hugh Glass rather than one of the other Mountain Men because his crawl was in South Dakota? Wasn't it the geographical location that determined the choice there?*

Well, to some extent, thank God that he did crawl in South Dakota. I looked at Colter, and I looked at Bridger, and at some of the others, but it seemed to me that Hugh Glass was the first really great hero we had. Ulysses . . . if you go back into Greek history, or into any of the other cultures, the heroes they celebrate most almost always do their big thing for what seems to me ulterior motives. That is, they have almost a selfish reason for what they did. Hugh Glass was a hero for larger reasons. He didn't do it for money. He didn't do it because he was ordered to by a commander. He didn't do it because he was part of an army. He didn't do it because his wife told him to do it. Or a minister of religion. He did it for the sake of an idea. The idea was at first a bad one, hate, but it was an idea. Then later on hate became love, or compassion, which was a still greater idea. You see, if you are doing something for the sake of an outside idea, not your own idea, but an outside idea, someone telling you to do it, or if you are a member of a religious organization and do it for the cause of the organization or a society, well, you have that to sustain you when you are really down. But Hugh, as low as he was, was alone. He was almost self-contained.

> *In fact, he made his first move because someone told him not to.*

Yes.

> *That is, leaving the group.*

Yes. And that seems to be rather authentic. That he did that. To me he is one of the world's first really great heroes.

Thank God we have him in the American society. Or in American history. I really should say there still wasn't much of an American society at that time. He made the American society by being there. That's why I was so delighted and happy to find him. About a month after *Lord Grizzly* was printed, I suddenly get a letter in the mail from William Carlos Williams. Out of the clear. I had met William Carlos Williams a few times, and I had visited with him, but I never expected that he would read any of my things. But someone gave him the book and his wife Flossie read it to him.[1] Each day they read a chapter, just as if they were reading from the Bible.[2] He wrote me this wonderful letter talking in terms of the *Iliad* and the *Odyssey*. And he mentioned that what I was looking at was not only an old-time hero, but a new hero, and our American hero, and a great man.

> *When you first began writing* Grizzly, *did you have in mind any of the themes and patterns that some of us have picked out since then?*

No, I think they emerged as I went along. I tried to visualize myself into his place. Of course we have some record of what he did from Chittenden. Ten pages. And little bits and jottles here and there from other people. Yount and so on. But I tried to imagine what this man would do. What I would do if I were there. And in the process of imagining this I went down to the bare essentials. To the biology of the thing. And of course the botany of it too. What the Old Lizard would do to survive. And out of that I would go along. And as I went along, these things did occur to me. I have seen these things which you mentioned, about the opening up of the consciousness, and going out and going up, stage by stage. All this was in my mind, but not before I began to write. I always sort of waited for things to emerge as I went along. I have somewhat the same attitude toward my material that Melville had. There is a story that Melville said, when he rewrote *Moby Dick* after Hawthorne told him he should do more with it — he then backed up and went all over it again and rewrote it —

[1] The truth is I had it sent to him. But I was surprised that he actually did read it. FFM

[2] Ha! FFM

when he was writing it, he always held his one hand, like this, to his face, sort of half-averted from the manuscript, and wrote it. If he looked too straight at it, the vision would vanish. But by having some of it sort of hidden from him, as if to let the unconscious write it, it would be richer and deeper. I have somewhat the same attitude toward this. I want to know as much as I possibly can, consciously and intellectually, about a subject. But when it comes time to write, then I turn my back on my more obvious knowledges. I turn my back on all previous theories on plot and previous theories on style, and I try to find the inner truth of what I am getting at. Not only my truth, but the truth about what is in the story. I turn my back as resolutely as I possibly can on all past endeavors, on all past writers, to be as completely and thoroughly myself as I can, and beyond that to be as thoroughly and completely the book I am doing as I can, as I have a feeling that no matter how original you are, you still are going to be somewhat near the last one to try it. It is difficult to be original. And you are not going to be original at all when you imitate or ape someone. I have gone to the point where I won't memorize a line of poetry for a time. If I find a song working in my head, I'll do everything I can to get it out of me. I don't want that rhythm telling me what to do. I want to do *my* rhythm. Find out what I am about. And that helps me find out what sits inside the book. It becomes the book's rhythm. So each book eventually finds its own voice. Finds its own existence. What's important is not me, but the book when I am done. Who gives a whoop about me? A hundred years from now they won't care. What counts is the book.

> *The one thing you did work on rather consciously, as I recall, is the ending, and this is the one thing that many readers don't like, the fact that Hugh will forgive the enemies he set out to kill. And this, as I recall, you said you got from an incident with one of your brothers.*

No, not my brother, but some relative. A distant relative of ours. He was falsely accused of something and the state pounced upon him. When we heard about it, of course (we were a good tight clan), we were willing to help, my lawyer brother and myself and the other brothers. We checked it all out and we thought, well, maybe it had happened. We were ready to accept it. But the further we looked into it the more we saw suddenly it wasn't true. Then came the day when the state had to back up and had to make an apology. And did. But some of the relatives said, "You ought to sue the state and make some money on this." But the man said, "No, they just made an honest error." And he just forgave them. I saw right in front of me a man forgiving another for a gross offense, which was just as serious as what happened to Hugh Glass. And now, since I was a piece of it, I then had the feel of it. You see, my problem with *Lord Grizzly* was . . . I wanted to do it. I had a pretty good vision of who Hugh was, and I knew pretty well how I wanted to handle it, but I didn't know how to end it. I knew I wanted him to forgive, but I didn't know how to do it completely and vividly. I wanted that to come out of my life-blood, so to speak, so it would be true when they really read it. That it would happen. Well, when I saw this in front of me, I then knew how to end it. Emotionally. Truly. Then I went after it. The moment I had that I went after it. Shortly after this experience came about, I went after it with hammer and tongs. Immediately. Before it was gone.

> *How do you account for the fact that many readers don't like the ending?*

Well, there are some that do like it.

> *Oh, yes, surely.*

Well, it's because I think that they are on about the same level as those relatives I have, the relatives who wanted this friend to sue and get some money out of it. They wanted exaction, not justice, just exaction. These readers have the same attitude. It's a low motive they have. When people tell me they don't like the ending, I know where to place them. They might be all right on some other occasion, but at that particular time they fall down in my estimation.

> *What about the argument that the ending as it exists is a letdown artistically, if you rule out the morality and the justice and consider it as art?*

I think they are flatly wrong. I think as time goes on . . . I think there is a case where the morality can be buried under the mask of artistic principles. Most people do hide what they do think under these artistic principles. They mask what they really feel. . . . And suppose it (the ending) *is* wrong? So what? It is still a good story. *Huckleberry Finn* is supposed to have a horrible ending. Everybody complains that Mark Twain should have ended it when they first hit . . . what is it, the state of Mississippi? . . . or at least down the river somewhere. And as far as that goes, what book is perfect? I can find all kinds of fault in *Hamlet*, in *Oedipus* by Sophocles, from my point of view. But that doesn't prove it wrong particularly. Each man makes as powerful a stab as he can and then he lets it go. And if people want to say, this is not good, that's their privilege. I have no objection.

> *Do you think Hugh Glass becomes a stronger figure, and even more ethical, because he can forgive?*

Of course. Because that's the final human summit that we have to climb to be human. You see, if we were all able to make this climb he made, we wouldn't even be making the thing.

> *In the book again, what about the preparation for the forgiveness? I recall parts of the book in which you have actually prepared the reader to accept this.*

Oh, yes. Well. Dutton returns and it puts Hugh's exploit into place. And More and Marsh and Chapman don't return. And Jim Clyman returns and he too puts Hugh's exploit into place. And then furthermore . . .

> *Fitz himself comes in there at the end.*

It all finally comes into place and this sets up Hugh's forgiveness of Fitz. But before that happens a very important thing occurs, and that is when Hugh is walking through the Badlands. There is this . . . I still don't know myself whether that was a real grizzly or a spiritual grizzly that was following Hugh down the White River.

Do a lot of people want to ask that?

I don't know myself. There were days when I thought that I was really describing a real one. And there were days when I thought I was describing a haunt-like grizzly. And since it happened that way, it's precisely a good thing, because it sets up a wondering in the reader's mind. Just as in the Bible when Jacob was wrestling with the Lord. Now an atheist or an agnostic says the Lord was not the Lord at all; it was just a fantasy that Jacob wrestled with the Lord at night, that made him lame and called him Israel. And then, of course, there are the very religious people who say that it was actually done. We still don't know which really was there. And so this is true of . . . I don't know . . . I didn't think about the wrestling of Jacob with the Lord at night at the time I was doing this book. Afterwards someone pointed this out to me. Maybe. I haven't read the Bible lately as much as I did when I was a boy. But maybe that did enter into my mind. There are so many things that play around in your mind when you are writing, it is almost impossible to put them down.

There are two patterns that in a sense contradict each other in the book. This will be interesting to hear about. You recall early in the novel when the Arikaras . . . or is it the Rees? . . .

The Rees.

. . . are attacking the Mountain Men, and as some of the Mountain Men die, there is a passage that says they looked inward and then looked outward and then they look inward again before they die. Now this, just by the proportions, would indicate that the individual is the important man, rather than the society around him.

Yes.

But in the overall pattern with Hugh Glass, he is mauled by the grizzly because he leaves the group and, although he survives as an individual, he has to go back to the group. Now, these two are just opposites.

This sounds like classroom to me. But now that I think about it, no, there is no conflict in my mind. I always had the feeling that a society is only as strong as its weakest individual, and the more powerful the individual the stronger the society. I don't believe . . . I myself feel that the inner-directed man makes for the powerful society. The other-directed man makes for mishmash and we have nothing. We have weaklings around us. There are a lot of them around today. So I feel . . . but it's probably old-fashioned . . . or rather new-fashioned . . . because in another generation I feel they are going to be emphasizing that we should be inner-directed, not other-directed.

But what if we were all like Hugh Glass? What kind of society would we have?

I grew up in that kind of a society as a young man and I thought it was great. Amongst farmers. Sure, you're going to have a few trash around. But so what? You're going to have more respect for a friend if he bites you once in a while, not intellectually, but if he bites you emotionally.

What I am trying to get at is whether Lord Grizzly *as a novel contributes something to the dilemma which Cooper pointed out in, for example,* The Prairie: *that it is good to have individualism; in fact, it is necessary; but it is also necessary to have an enlightened society. How do we resolve this?*

An enlightened society is where strong individuals learn to tolerate each other as individuals. The whole trick is to raise an ego that other people will tolerate. Not to raise non-egos. But the whole trick of education, of having a family, everything, is to raise egos. There is no harm in the word "ego." To raise egotists that other people will tolerate. Because man is both a gregarious creature and he is a solitary creature. No one can help you inside your own skull, inside the envelope of your skin. Whatever condition you find in there, that's you. There isn't much they can do actually to tinker around inside of that. But what you do with other envelopes next to you may help you live a little happier. I myself like to see a society of strong individualists who learn to get along.

> *Does this relate to the point of view that is used in the novel too? Do you recall that a professor at the University of Minnesota once objected to a couple of passages in which Hugh was said to have stinky leathers on that smelled like bear grease, et cetera, and contended that Hugh would not think these things about himself?*

Well, he was wrong about that. In the first place, an author doesn't bother to say I am going to use this point of view or that point of view. Every man has a way of living from moment to moment in relation to his environment, and he has various ways of getting at it, accepting it, and seeing it. And so each person also has to work out his own way of writing. You can't say that there is this kind of point of view and so-and-so writes according to it, so therefore you should do it that way too. I don't believe that. If there are one hundred writers there will be a hundred ways of doing it. I happened to do it this way. It works for me. This is the way I regard life and therefore it works. It is a valid point of view. And as I have noticed, sometimes I am totally immersed as a person in a spot. And then there are times when only part of me is immersed while another piece of me is sitting up here recording all of this and checking it out, saying, "Well, I don't know if I want this now or not." In other words, someone sitting sort of behind my eyeballs. And then there is further back what I call the Old Lizard who really watches the whole show, or the Old Goat who is really boss of everything. So when I am writing it depends upon which one of these fellows is talking through me. Sometimes it's the guy back here that is working; sometimes it's the guy that's here, just behind over here; and then there is the guy that's just behind the eyeballs alone. As long as people read the book and are absorbed in it, it works. That's it. The heck with these theories. I don't pay much attention to them . . . . This is the point. If within a given endeavor the work is more or less consistent and doesn't jump around too much and isn't too fluttery, that's it. Then it works. I am suspicious of all these theories about what to do. I know what they mean. And there are times when I am exasperated with an author because he isn't sure in whose mind he is sitting. He jumps all around the place. But that person doesn't really know where he himself is living. That kind of a guy probably has accidents; prone to have accidents. Maybe has trouble with his wife. Because he doesn't know who he is really. So he has a lousy point of view in any case, with his wife, or in letters.

> *We have pointed out the various kinds of patterns in* Grizzly. *Have you ever counted all the threes? There are three parts to the novel. And in a number of places you have passages arranged in groups of three. I recall once when Hugh is sleeping with the soughing of the wind. And three passages repeating in a rather biblical style the natural description at that point when three Mountain Men come in from the wilderness. This forms a pattern. Nothing conscious in the threes?*

There was probably a "three" at work. Because in our society we have this fetish of threes. Baseball, three outs, which I play a lot of. Father, mother and children, there's a three. And three generations generally, you know, your father and mother and yourself and Grandma and Grandpa. Three runs heavily back into prehistoric times. So this is continually at work in any given person. But that I thought of this and consciously put them in the book, no. I can't say that I really realized that. It's difficult for me to recall everything that was at work in me on a given day of writing. It is difficult to remember everything that was in your mind as you worked along. You can only remember main things. I will say this, though. It always amuses me just a little bit that . . . here I had Hugh Glass in my head some ten years off and on, on the back of the stove, so to speak, and did a lot of thinking about it in casual moments, sometimes directly and sometimes indirectly, and then I finally spent a whole year researching it and then a year writing it, so that by this time I am so thoroughly immersed in it all every day that I wrote — I'd spend a little time going over some thirty pages of collected dialogue from ancient times which I thought was authentic and I would read that the first thing in the morning to get this rhythm going, because it has a syntax of its own — after all that, and knowing as much as I do, and also being a pretty good friend of Old Man Unconscious, who I like, and being a pretty good friend of the Old Dreamer back there, and the Old Lizard, and knowing when He is saying, "Well, okay, go ahead and write it," or, "Don't write it," how, after all that, one man sitting down, say, one evening and reading the book can write a review and tear it all to pieces . . . that amuses me. His knowledge of that book can't begin to compare with what I know about it. So offhand I would just say that he's wrong, or he's right. But at the time *I* really knew. I was the real critic, wrong or right.

> *You mentioned reading older books for dialogue. Do you recall whether it was Ruxton or Garrard that you took? Did you take both equally?*

Yes. And I took a few others too. Yount. He wrote some things on a slate and then he dictated the rest to his daughter. A very old man. She took it down and it was printed in a California Historical Society bulletin. There were some fine things in that. And *Forty Years in the Fur Trade* by Larpenteur. There were quite a few authentic records of the day. If you want to look for it you can find these ancient words and phrases. I sometimes read as much as fifty pages to get one phrase right. When I'd find a good phrase I'd keep it. I'd decide this was it.

> *Do you remember at all the total number of books you read in preparing for* Lord Grizzly? *I think you told me once sixty.*

Oh no, more than that. About a hundred. . . . Well, actually a hundred that I digested thoroughly and then maybe about another hundred that I looked at. And then quite a few articles in magazines. Garrard and Ruxton, I really soaked those up. They were authentic. They were young men. Their minds, their memories were good. And they were vivid writers. They loved it all and they got the spirit of it.

> *Now, is it true that almost every character in* Lord Grizzly *is historically accurate except perhaps Bending Reed? Is she the only invented person?*

Yes. Though I now understand that Yount wasn't with Hugh on that trip. I find out that a guy named Black Harris was there instead of Yount. One error there in my book, according to the historians. But I am going to accept that. I suppose ten years from now they will turn that picture around and say that Yount was there after all. But Bending Reed was somebody that I invented and put in there. I did know that most Mountain Men had girl friends, that they (the Mountain Men) were related to a tribe, that they married into a tribe. Once they were a part of the tribe they had protection. They were often invited, in fact, to marry into the Indian tribes. So I gave him Bending Reed. There is no evidence, as far as I know, that the real Hugh had a Bending Reed.

No, I hadn't seen any.

I don't know of any. They said he was an old man and maybe that accounts for it. But they don't say much about Bridger's girl friend either.

No.

In his youth. Or for that trip. So . . . Reed came to me fleetingly in real life after I'd already had her down in the first draft of *Lord Grizzly*. I was up at Fort Berthold to check out some of the detail of that first draft. I had a date to meet an old Arikara chief, and as I walked across the Fort grounds there were two Indian girls trying to get into a cabin. They were having trouble with the key. So I paused and looked over a little bit, and I asked them, "What seems to be the trouble here?" And this prettiest one said, "Well, we can't seem to get the key in." This was interesting. So I took the key and I felt for the weights in the lock and, sure enough, she hadn't gone in deep enough. Then I turned it and it opened. A little later when I'd finished talking with the old chief and came by her cabin again, she came out to ask me something. It turns out that her friend who was with her suddenly couldn't go along with her. They'd meant to go to a dance together. The two girls were going to drive to an Indian dance up at New-town. And so just sort of naturally, almost as if it had been my cousin, she asked if . . .

The Buckskin Man Tales, five volumes altogether, depict various phases of the old American West. Now within that series of five, we might point out that one of them, Riders of Judgment, *is a cowboy novel. Walter Clark in 1940 created quite a stir with* The Ox-Bow Incident *because he had presumably done a cowboy novel that was realistic. He got rid of all the romance and all the heroic cowboys who could do anything. But there still are hundreds of cowboy novels around and when you set out to do one now as you have with* Riders of Judgment, *how do you feel that you can contribute anything more to this mass, or mess, of literature that already exists? Have you done another* Ox-Bow?

I don't know. I really didn't give it much thought worrying about whether or not all that had been done. As a boy I remember reading Westerns occasionally in the drugstore on Saturday afternoon. It occurred to me at that time that I would like to do one that was true. I always had the feeling that there was something false about them. Or invented. Usually invented by people living in Brooklyn who had never been west of the Hudson. And also I had the dream as a young boy that I wanted to become a cowboy for a couple of years. This was in my head. And I did try to write a cowboy story as a kid once. But I always had it in my head that someday, after I knew something about the craft of writing, and I had studied a little the few books that had been written about the West, that I would go after that and really put it down. It was always my feeling that the real story hadn't been told. Even *The Virginian* I thought was somewhat artificial. It's ... it's a good one. There was an attempt there to put it down as it was. But even that is artificial.

That goes back far enough so one can excuse it perhaps.

Well, in those days they had their own notions about what should or should not go into a book. And he (Owen Wister) was somewhat of an eastern gentleman. The custom then was to be a gentleman officially, but privately one could be a villain and nobody talked about it. You weren't supposed to put the villain aspect into a book. I hadn't read Clark's *The Ox-Bow Incident* before I did *Riders of Judgment*. I had looked at it one day and decided that I better not read it. I might be pulled over. I am very impressionable. Any man worth his salt as a writer is impressionable. That's how he gets his material. So if he reads people who work near him, they will probably affect him a lot. As I said the other day, I try to turn my back on everything that has ever been done. So I didn't look at *The Ox-Bow Incident*. I have now read it since. A couple of times in fact. . . . I wanted to rediscover that boyhood dream. And I wanted . . . . If you're going to do a picture of the Old Far West, this would have to be a piece of it, the Cattleman Times. I finally decided to choose a date at a time when it was about ready to fade out, when the cattle empires were breaking up. The cause of the breakup, of course, was your nesters. Plus the railroads coming through, et cetera . . . I might tell you I had . . . in the beginning I didn't quite know what I was going to go after here either. I knew the general area. But in reading this book *The Banditti of the Plains*, there was a little story in there about a Nate Champion, and this caught my eye. As it stood it was a little awkward as a story. As to content. It didn't balance off. I had some problems there. I didn't know how to end it. Or where to begin it. Just before I began to write it I took a trip with my wife, first to Denver, where I checked out the library over there, and then to Cheyenne, and then to Casper, and then up to Kaycee. When I was in Cheyenne I stopped to see an archivist, Lola M. Homsher, I think her name is, at the State Archives and Historical Department, and she showed me some of the Nate Champion material they had. They are supposed to have a gun of his there. And the gun that is supposed to have killed him. She gave me the name of a woman who lived up in Kaycee who was doing some writing for her, a Mrs. Condit. Thelma Condit. Whose husband was a rancher, and perhaps three or four generations back whose ancestors were part of the bunch that broke up the big ranches.

This is around Buffalo, Wyoming?

Yes, Kaycee is below Buffalo. Between Buffalo and Casper. It's still a rough wild town. They still have the white owl under the bed instead of the urinal in the bathroom down the hall. And the hotels there, they have such wonderful names as The Feed Rack, Invasion Bar. The Invasion Bar commemorates this big invasion of the big-time cattlemen and their gunmen from Texas. My wife and I drove over to see Mrs. Condit and talked to her for a while. She was pleasantly warm. But cagey. She wasn't sure she wanted to tell me what she knew. After all, she didn't know me. The last thing I said to her as we left the house that evening was, "Well, if you won't tell me about him, it will just be the book's loss, and Nate Champion's loss, since I'm going to write about him anyway. So you might just as well tell me what you know." Well, the next morning I came back there around nine o'clock. She said, "Well, I've had a sleepless night and I've decided to tell you everything I know." Among other things she told me that Nate Champion had actually been killed some twenty rods from her house right out in the open flat there toward the creek. She showed me some of his things. She told me that among other things the gun they had down at Cheyenne wasn't Nate's true gun, that his real gun was in the hands of the family. She said people. I'd had some trouble finding pictures of Nate Champion. There is one they have but it is hard to make out. But she said that the family has a trunkful of stuff of his. I said, "Does the State Historical Department know this?" She said, "No, they don't. I haven't dared to tell them yet." Well, I was eager to get hold of that material. But she said, "There's no chance. They're still fighting that war." While we were talking there was a rap on the door and here comes a car full of people up. It turns out that they were the Tisdales who are cousins of the Champions. The oldest member there, Johnny Tisdale, famous rodeo champion, was about to be born the day that Nate Champion was killed and he (Nate) was to be his godfather. That's as close as I could get. Because we were sitting and talking with Mrs. Condit, and seemed to be on easy terms with her, the Tisdales assumed that we were of the ins, friends, so they kept telling all day long about what they had come there for, to commemorate and talk over the old days. She, Mrs.

Condit, wanted to write an article about them, and they drove some forty to fifty miles from behind the Red Wall at the foot of the Big Horns, they drove in to talk to her about this. And so all day long they talked about Nate Champion and the boys. Stuff was coming at me so fast I had my mind's camera, my antennae out too far, so I was getting in too much too fast. So I pleaded that I had a slightly uneasy stomach and bad kidneys, and as often as I could I would go to the bathroom and I'd scribble notes like mad in there. They probably thought I really was a sick man. Then that night, of course, I dug into my wife's memory to get that down as much as I could. To show you the wonderful humor they have . . . there is a little Texas in Wyoming people, for after all the Texas cowboys settled up there and brought their ways up with them. My wife wanted to make some conversation with Johnny Tisdale, who didn't say very much. They are very polite, they have courtly manners about them. They have their boots on, manure-spattered boots, you know, but courtly. My wife asked him, to make some conversation, "Tell me, Mr. Tisdale, have you lived here all your life?" He says, "Not yit." I always thought that was very funny. That was the kind of humor that went on all day long. Which I delighted in. And I took as many notes as possible. So the conversation that I have in *Riders of Judgment* is based a lot on this conversation I heard out there in Kaycee. The next day I had an interesting experience. Johnny Tisdale's niece was a graduate from the journalism school at Laramie, Wyoming, and I was told that she was the one who had been entrusted with the Nate Champion material. She was the custodian of this big trunk. They told me that there was no chance of ever getting into it because she was a strong-headed, bull-headed woman, with eyes wide apart. Which I thought was a great description. But very pretty. I drove up there to her home in Buffalo. I decided to tackle this bull-headed woman, and I knocked on the door, and she opened it and looked at me a little coldly. I said, "I am so-and-so, and I talked to Thelma Condit and your uncle Johnny Tisdale, and I know you folks are touchy about this, but I am going to write about Nate Champion. You may come shooting for me some day, which is all right with me, but while we are at it, why don't you just give me as much information as you can?" She stood there for a minute, literally a full minute, just staring at me, trying to stare me down. It didn't work, of course. Because a writer has more than enough guts when he wants something. You know, almost rude. She finally invited me in. I saw right away that she was going to be a mother soon. Her husband was gone on the road somewhere. We talked for a little while and finally she said, "You know, the family gave this trunk to me, this trunk full of materials, for me to protect. Also they thought that maybe someday I should do something with it, since I have learned to write a little. Now, I can't show this to you. But I can do one thing. I can show you where Nate Champion is buried." So we got in her car and we drove out to the cemetery on the edge of Buffalo, and she showed me Nate's grave and how they took care of it, and of Nate's brother's grave, et cetera. That really brought it home. You know, seeing this girl who was going to have a baby, an unborn baby at just about the same stage when Johnny Tisdale was going to be born at the time of Nate's death . . . it all sort of nicely fell in together. That book is based on more reality than people might know. It really is in there, and to me it is as close as you could come to what happened. This is the way it was.

> *Is this now what really makes it valuable to you, making it accurate?*

Yes, as the groundwork. Then, of course, I would like to think there is a little order in it too. You know, construction, building, the way it is all put together. And the language of the day. The true language.

> *What I am thinking about is the major concern with doing this particular Johnson County range war incident. We think of A. B. Guthrie trying to recreate the West, the Mountain Man, the covered wagons on the Oregon Trail, et cetera. Is this finally what the cowboy novel will probably have to come to? Reestablishing the realism?*

Yes.

> *Instead of the myth?*

On top of that . . . well, let the myth enter after the realism is made. Let the plot and the construction, et cetera, enter just as if you were to go back to Grecian times. I like to go back to the Greeks. They had realism too. They really dug it out. But handling it over and over again for several hundred years they finally worked out basic human concerns, kept them alive, and then shaped them into real works of art. In addition to realism we should also get some sort of . . . well, I should say mental construction, get something into it that the higher reaches of our personality will be satisfied to look at.

Isn't there a temptation to take sides when you are dealing with an historic incident like this? Do you sympathize now, for example, with Cain Hammett?

Yes. You see, Nate Champion became Cain Hammett. I changed their names. I might tell you why I changed names. In *Lord Grizzly* I kept Hugh Glass as a name because there wasn't much on him. Soon I found that Hollywood was interested in buying *Lord Grizzly*, but they wanted to buy it for chicken feed. I knew that to sell it cheap would be a mistake. Because when everybody'd hear that I had sold to Hollywood they'd have me rich, as they say, and they would overcharge me. The five or ten thousand dollars that I might get for it would disappear in a half year, and then I'd be one of those writers who went Hollywood and still was broke. All the Hollywood people wanted to do was buy the title from me and so get rid of me. Because, they said, they could go to the history to get the story. Well, that taught me a lesson. Since then there have been some other books about Nate Champion with the name Nate in it. And there's been one other novel. I didn't read it; have never read it. It was written by some woman. I forget who she is now.

Had she gotten close to the family though?

No. She used only what was generally known so far and what was in this book *The Banditti of the Plains* by Mercer. What was your question?

Whether your sympathies were with Cain Hammett entirely, because this amounts to taking a stand.

Well, no. Privately I might have been on their side. I have been so much for the underdog all my life. It's a funny thing — I am in sympathy with the underdog but I get along best with the upperdog. The upperdog has read a few books and the underdog hasn't. So that's a real dichotomy in a man's life. I usually get around to where I can see the other side pretty well too. I tried to portray the other side the best I could. After all, they were losing their empires. They did build the West to begin with. They set everything up and they took great chances, the original cattlemen and cattle barons. They took tremendous chances. They took other people's money and invested it and it really was a rough go. But in this particular area that I spoke of, in the Big Horns, the valleys were narrow and long, and it made a perfect setup for small ranches, not big ones. It happens that the cattle barons were losing a lot of cattle in those canyons. They were disappearing over those sides. While the small man could easily tend to one little valley, one canyon, one draw. The small men did have a point there. That it would be put to better use. Also, my own feeling is outside money really doesn't have any place in America. It was outside money which made your representatives for these absentee cattle barons do these things to the cowboys who wanted a setup of their own. I am all for . . . England is fine, and Europe is fine and all that, but I am all for America to begin with. I won't say it is the best, but it happens to be where I am, and where I live, and so I want that.

Well, you were fairly objective actually in Riders of Judgment *right up until the last chapter and the funeral. I remember you once said that you had been waiting for a long time to hear a good funeral sermon, and then it comes out just a little bit that the puff of smoke was like Sinclair Lewis's service in Sauk Center.*

Say, I wonder if that had anything . . . I'll bet it did, the day I gave the eulogy.

Yes, it was cold.

It was twenty below.

The ashes had been indoors and so sent up a little puff of smoke.

Mark Schorer is all wrong about that, by the way, saying that the ashes flew all over the prairie. Actually it was when they took Lewis's ashes, when they opened the urn and poured the ashes all over his books that were in this cut hole in the frozen ground, that that warmth difference of ninety degrees made a kind of an explosion of steam. Of vapor. I suppose that had something to do with it. I . . . that thought was working on me. I did have in mind, as you've noticed . . . . The book begins in a cloud and ends in a cloud. Just as if this man came down to earth for a little while, and did these things, and made a sacrifice, and went back up again.

It makes the frame of the book somewhat mythical but the middle is realistic.

Yes, that is what I wanted. But the frame, the cloud, though, that is realistic too. When you go into the Big Horns, if you have ever driven up to the top you are often driving in the clouds. And I think some people are born sort of mysteriously to families. Ordinary families all of a sudden have a genius in the family.

Now, the novel Conquering Horse *is based on an historical incident, is it not?*

No. Well, it is true that the Indians have sun-dances. It is true that the Indian had these things that *Conquering Horse* has.

But since this goes back earlier in historical times, didn't you have to invent more, as it were?

Yes. Oh yes. I had to do an enormous amount of invention. I had quite a problem there, quite a task. It really was a challenge, that one. I wanted to get it as true as I could get it, too. I wasn't too sure I could handle Indian themes, or the Indian way of thinking, and I wasn't too sure that there was material for a book that a white man would or could read. Because in a certain sense, you know, that book should never have been written. An Indian hadn't been developed enough yet — at least they certainly hadn't at that time — to organize a work of literature. And at the same time, a white man shouldn't know that much about an Indian. It shouldn't have been written. I had a real problem there. I had to get in between those two and do it. But as I went along I remembered the few Indian boys I had known as a child. And I found myself in great sympathy with Indians whenever I met them at Pine Ridge and at the Cheyenne River Indian Reservation in western South Dakota. When people told me that the Indians that'd shown up in *Lord Grizzly* felt real to them and true, I thought then, well, I can probably do it. I thought — in our society young men aren't receiving the laying on of hands any more. And the test of manhood in a trial by fire — we don't have that any more. Whereas the Indians did. And the early white man did too. And I thought that this would be a great chance to explore this business of trial by fire by a youth.

> *Did you live with Indians at all as Frank Waters has done recently?*

No. I went on the theory that I shouldn't go too much into it. They always say that the first time in you always give a better impression than the tenth time in. They say you have to go a hundred times into a thing before you are as good as you are the first time. Something goes on in that first motion. If you got your antennae out, and your brain is raw and open, that first impact is usually a true one. Almost like a child's impression of a stranger.

> *Well now, again, besides simply recreating some facts of the Old West, what are you trying to say in* Conquering Horse, *if anything?*

Well, I don't set out to write a book to say something. And I say this again, because so often people think "This man set out to say this." Critics do this so often. You don't. The truth is that he was *moved* to do something. He is *moved* to go into an area. It is appealing to him. He can't get it out of his head. Well, that's reason enough to write a book. . . . Justice, for one thing, was going on in my head. We have really stolen this land from the Indians. Just taken it away from him. And in some respects some parts of the Indian world were equal to ours. If not superior. The Mayas, who developed a tremendous civilization. And we destroyed that. Wiped it out as much as we could. I have probably a white man's sense of guilt. But I feel I should pay these people our respects. We are living on their land. They were already adjusted to it and used to it. They were a piece of it. The land and they were one. We are not. Pier isn't a piece of the land like the Indians were. He hasn't really become a man who is at home in his country. So I wanted to show how the Indian lived at that time. Why he did what he did. His beliefs and his fate came up out of the land. You see, I think people, people tend to be the voice of the land. And the white man, even today, isn't the voice of our American land. Just a few of us guys are trying to do it. Fisher. And Waters and Clark. Faulkner. Lewis didn't. Dreiser didn't either, really. Every country develops a voice. I mean, every soil develops a voice through its people. Through its animal life and through its people. And so I felt that if this country was to have a voice, somebody better let the Indians talk before the knowledge of them vanished entirely. I had some of it, so I had better do it. Also it makes good writing.

Yes, it does.

And I would like to have it that when the Americans get through reading my books, reading them thoroughly, even the squeamish people who should read those realistic sections of my books that make them jump, when they get all done, I want them to feel that they have been there. That's what I want to do if possible.

You know Oliver La Farge's Laughing Boy. *Now, that one is slightly propagandistic.*

La Farge is arguing, shoving it.

You mean that the Indian got a dirty deal, and as a result, La Farge sentimentalizes the Indian a little bit. Now you have had nothing like that in mind, and probably tried to avoid it.

Avoid it, yes. Avoid propaganda. Let it stand. Let it kindle by itself.

And the other one that comes to mind is Waters again. The Man Who Killed the Deer. *Now, there is a sense of justice, but within the Indian tribe as well as between the Indians and the whites.*

It's a little different. Well, he lived more thoroughly with them.

Do you think that the mere historical accuracy of, say, the Buckskin Man Tales is enough to justify them, even before the professor begins reading things into them? I am thinking of Guthrie now, you know . . .

Yes. Well maybe so.

. . . who does something of that kind.

I like to have it be more than that, of course. I am not interested in just recording history. I am a novelist to begin with. To me, to be a novelist, if I can accept that term "novel" . . . I have a little trouble accepting it . . . well, let's say, a fictionist . . . to be a writer of fiction is to work at the most difficult of all the arts. Of all the human endeavors it's the noblest. So I want not only to be a good fiction writer, I also want to make a contribution in that field if I possibly can.

What would you say if an English professor took No Name *out of* Conquering Horse *and said, "Here is an example of the American who has no name, no tradition, he is innocent, and he has to find a place for himself." Would this suit you?*

Well, if he has a good time with it, let him do it. I don't care. I was interested in the "no name" business because people do try to find their identity. Who they are. In all times, in all languages, in all countries, and on all planets. Who they are. In the beginning they are born with no name. And with Indians you earn your name. We Americans just slap any old name on our kids, you know. Named after some relative without any rime or reason, actually. Anne Feikema.* Who came out of Europe where the names they had there meant something. But in this country it is just sort of empty. I was quite concerned about that. To me it means something to know what Manfred means. And it means something to know what Frederick means. It means, among other things, head of the house. And I want my first boy to be a real head of the house someday. The name-*track*, I want that to mean something. So, No Name. This was an expression of this problem.

> *And you have answered my question now too. Because you have suggested something broad or significant that comes out of the novel and out of the Indian customs.*

* Anne is Frisian and is usually Anglicized as meaning Andrew. FFM

The man who published Morning Red, *Alan Swallow, in some ways indicated that he thinks it is your big one. But when it first came out a very dear friend of ours, John Sherman in Minneapolis, panned it to a certain extent, and, as I recall, partly because he didn't find some of the incidents believable or plausible, the tornado picking the coupe up and setting it down without blowing the tires, the tongueless woman below the bridge, and similar incidents. When you get criticism like that from a very good friend, which John is, what does that tend to do to you? Do you have any doubts that you made the book plausible?*

No. No, because by this time, you see, I have gone through the wringer having made it. I know what I put into it and I know what I had in mind. Naturally, you like to have your friends like it. But on the other hand I know that my friends are not me. They are different from me in many respects. And this is a free country, so they have a right to their opinion. I was a little distressed by that review because I . . . for one reason, *Morning Red* was printed by a small publisher in Denver who didn't have a sales force. Whereas the people in New York have a great sales force. Swallow had taken a lot of his own pocket money, so to speak, and put it into something that he loved. A bad review might hurt the sales of it, which disturbed me some. I don't mind so much a bad review for a New York publisher since he is big enough to survive a disaster. But Swallow, who has been printing mostly poets and some criticism, could ill afford a tumbling collapse in the matter of one book. But, more, it is the duty of a writer, if he knows something, to put it down. And I don't mean just realistically but put it down with some form and style. He must not back away from his knowledges and his notions of truth. To duck and to hide. I wondered just a little bit if John Sherman wasn't a little bit overly concerned about the kinds of friends he has or meets at parties, et cetera. If he were to write very friendly about it, then these people would be upset and they would sort of get after him. If he wasn't sort of protecting his own position. But I was more worried about something else. I wanted that book to have an audience. It had a right to talk on its own whether I wrote it or anybody else wrote it. It had a right to be read despite what Sherman said. That's why . . . I think that's the only time I ever wrote a public remonstrance to a critic, and in a rather warm way. I didn't dress him down or anything. I really explained why I wrote the book, and why I was writing the letter. I tried to tell him that the real truth was that I hadn't really poured an awful lot of darkness and sadness into the book, that it (life) really was much worse than I'd put into the book, that I'd carefully balanced it all out, that it really was a piece of representation, representative good and bad. The funny thing about that book is that since then many of the things that I described in it have occurred in Minneapolis. Gangsterism. There have been a number of rapes since then. Tornadoes transporting cars. And some of the politics that I described has happened. One important family has had a big scandal. It hasn't gotten into the papers, but most of the people in the city now talk about it. This I had in the book. I have a friend who comes from the Mt. Curve–Summit Avenue bunch who can't quite believe that I knew so much about them. He says, "Where did you learn all this? It happens to be true." And that that one very rich and influential man should be playing both sides of the line, which is something he didn't know that I knew either. But he knew it. And it is common knowledge amongst the in-group . . . I also got a rather sharpish letter from Malcolm Cowley on that.

On Morning Red?

Yes. Well, rather he and I had met one time, and he wrote me that one of the reasons why Viking Press, for whom he was a reader, didn't take it was that it wasn't a true picture of the rich in the Midlands. He said in the East the rich stand apart from the poor by their style and their Ivy League offishness and aloofness, et cetera. I explained to him that out in the Midlands that wasn't quite so true. Even the boys that go to Princeton for a while, when they come back to Minneapolis, they'd better shed some of that or they won't survive back here. You can go to a picnic or a fair or a baseball game and it is pretty hard to tell a rich man from a poor man. You can pick out a doctor and a professor, perhaps, in a crowd, but it is pretty hard to pick out a rich man. The rich and the poor tend to hunt together and you can't tell them apart. In fact, the poor man often has the best clothes on on a hunting trip, whereas the rich man is a little casual about it. Then he (Cowley) complained that the language wasn't quite right either. And there I defied him. I think I am a very fine recorder of what people say and do. I spend a lot of time taking it down and getting it accurate.

Was this just the language of the rich he objected to?

Yes.

Or all language?

Oh no, just the rich. He accepted the language of the poor. He made me smile a little bit. He doesn't know either one of them out here, so why should he accept the poor man's language? We exchanged some letters on this, some rather sharpish ones, and he kind of wound up trying to laugh in the last one. He said that every society on earth has had at one time or another a hierarchy. The moment you get society, hierarchy is developed. Well, I agree with that. But we still, though, try in the West to have a hierarchy based on worth, value, rather than by birth. Worth rather than by birth. You have to earn it out here. So the momentum of it staying in one family is less apt to happen out here than in the East. I suppose in time it will occur and I am describing this in some of my books.

I wonder if part of the problem here is just that critics come to expect the same kind of book from a writer time after time, and they became accustomed to you as a recorder of Iowa or South Dakota, and here was a metropolitan novel taking

place in Minneapolis, and maybe they just as-
sumed this wasn't your material.

Also they assumed that since no one else had dug
up this stuff it wasn't there. Two things worked against me. You
see, they had their own notions in the East of how we should be
doing things out here. And of course they are almost ninety percent wrong. And sometimes more than that. I had a terrible tough
time with that book. I was with McGraw-Hill who did *Lord
Grizzly*. Fine house. But they wanted me to do a new so-called
Western next and I wasn't ready. I don't want to write a thing
unless I am ready to do it. I had *Morning Red* ready and I sent it
in to them. My own editor, Bartlett, he would have gone along
with me, I think, but he was outvoted by Ed Aswell. Ed Aswell
was a Wolfe man. You remember Wolfe jumped from Perkins to
Aswell. And Aswell was overly concerned . . . now, if I would have
had Perkins for an editor I would have had no problem. Perkins
would have taken me for what I was. But I think that Aswell . . .
God bless his soul, the poor man has passed on . . . you hate to speak
this way about the dead . . . but I think that he was being overly
protective of the Wolfe image and he didn't like it that I was as
big as I was and moved around the way Wolfe did in some ways
physically. And possibly that I might even be a better writer. I
had more control, more restraint, and probably knew more than
Wolfe. I'd read better and had a better notion of true dialogue
and true plotting, et cetera. He knew my opinion of Wolfe. He'd
asked me if I had read Wolfe, and I'd said, "I can't read him."
Well, I really hurt myself there terribly with him. At any rate he
belittled *Morning Red*. He told me to shelve it. Imagine! He
told me to shelve that book. Well, then we brought it to a few other
houses.[1] Knopf. And I forget the other ones. And finally . . . I
remember one house. This is the kind of thing they told me to do.
They told me either take out the Jack Nagel business or else take
out the Kurt Faber idea. That the two characters made for separate books. You could almost pick out who was what by what they
would ask me to do in this respect.

Which plot they wanted taken out.

[1] My agent Alan Collins and I. FFM

You could always pick out who they were, what kind of intelligence they had, what kind of a person they were. In fact, I use that as a judgment stone, this book. How people react to this book tells me an awful lot about them, who is talking to me. I never gave up on it, though. I knew I was right. Now, I'll admit that that book in my own eyes has many major defects. It was a book where I dove deep and then tried to rise as high as I could. At the same time. It was the first time I'd ever really made such an exploration of that type. And the first time . . . you don't always swim the river the right way the first time. You have to learn your river. To swim across the best places and to learn where the fords are and where the bank isn't too steep to get up the other side. And all that. But I finally wrote a note to Alan Swallow. I'd heard about him in Denver. I'd heard that he was printing Western poets and that he was interested in Western letters. I asked him if he would mind if I dropped by some day, and he said, "No, fine," so we did drop by.[2] They were reading the book in New York at the time. I forget who had it at the moment. And he said, "Well, someday when it comes back, why don't you send it to me?" So I finally did. To my great joy, about a month later he wrote me a long exciting letter about *Morning Red*. He said, "I don't want to change anything in it. Just leave it go as it is. I might argue about a little phrase here and there, but, after all, the phrase that I'd supplant it with is no better than the one you have. You have your name on it, so it should be yours." And that's how Swallow printed that book. It probably cost him a lot of money. He still probably hasn't got his money back on it.

I doubt it very much.

Although each year it is selling a little better.

And in the paperback series now some schools are beginning to use it.

Yes. I see the royalty statements and every six months it's climbing just a little more. And foreign sales are creeping in now. So it's alive. You see, it was printed in 1956. Eight years ago. Well, then she's in, even though the sales are still poor.

[2] My wife and I. FFM

These people who objected to the double plots, did any of them mention specifically that it was Monk who stands between them?

Well, I have a friend who did privately. He didn't publicly. Russell Roth. Real good friend, Russell. Who was a really wonderful mentor for me in some ways. At least he was a real good sounding-board. I often talk to him, when I don't talk to you. He was curious to know if this Monk fellow wasn't my Christ figure. He made a remark once that every author raised in Christendom eventually tends somewhere along the line to have one Christ figure. And he wanted to know if this wasn't my Christ figure. I hadn't thought of it that way. My feeling was that Monk, to do what he had to do, had to be a man who had been emasculated somewhere along the line. But brilliant. Had to be both a lawyer (not just a money-minded lawyer, but a justice-minded lawyer) and had to know something about psychology to understand what this boy Jack Nagel was like. You see, by having Monk be a monk as a man, he was a shade further down the scale of masculinity, so to speak, than Jack was. This helped set Jack up against the other backdrop characters as being savable. He still could be saved. Monk was quite a bit of an invention. Although I did see a public defender in action in the Twin Cities. I followed one case from beginning to end. A young boy of Russian descent, a wonderful lad, accidentally killed his wife who was about to have a baby, and all the Swedes and Scandinavian in-laws ganged up on him in the trial and he went under. Yet he was a pathetic fellow. He was a high school graduate who wrote poetry. He was in the Korean War and was sent home because he was too sensitive to be in the war, too delicate a flower. He was so open and so honest, so naïve, so childlike. When they asked him questions, he had no sense of guardedness. He just let everything fly. He would cry once in a while and the defense lawyer, Scoop Lohmann, who defended him, had quite a time setting up shields. Whereas the opposition, the prosecuting attorney . . . you know, they have a whole staff and a lot of money . . . they had the courtroom full of pictures of this young wife of his who'd been killed, blood all over, her naked body on the bed, you know, staring right at the jury. And he had nothing on his side. He was utterly defenseless. And he wound up in Stillwater. And, I thought, with no real justification. I think that there was a case where a boy . . . where there really was an injustice done. She (his wife) was the one who brought the knife into the bedroom and then they had a scuffle over it. He took it away from her. A little later she brought it back once again. Well, if I were on the jury, I would say right there it was the woman's fault. And, they were scuffling over this fact: his mother-in-law. He didn't want her around so much because she disturbed them. His wife tended to be bossy and find fault with him with the mother-in-law around. But after the mother-in-law had stayed away for a while, then she (his wife) was loving and his companion again. Her mother hated him and wanted to get rid of him. He was fighting an evil and had the right to do it. Well, this all intrigued me and I followed the whole case all the way through. Scoop did act a little bit in some instances like Monk did . . . . And I think maybe Monk is also a side of me.

He has his difficulties, is it in South Dakota?

No. Before he moves to Minneapolis. No, he was from Rock Rapids, Iowa. What I call Rock Falls. You see, of those things that I described . . . he was tarred and feathered, et cetera, and emasculated . . . those things happened in Orange City, Iowa, I understand, in the old days. And in Primghar and some of those places. But I moved them up over there (to Rock Falls). It is still typical of what could happen in the old days. And I wanted a man from the area who would have a clear eye and wouldn't have been bent too much by the city.

> *Bringing them in from the outside almost suggests that these two Minneapolis boys (Jack Nagel and the Russian boy) need that kind of help.*

Yes.

I don't know if you intended that or not.

Maybe I did. I sometimes think that . . . well, look what happens. Most of your leaders in the big cities tend to come from the country. Very occasionally do you have a local man (from

New York) make good in New York, for example. You can walk down the street and pick a prominent man and where does he come from? Most invariably it is from the outside. This is true in the arts, and in the entertainment world, and also in the . . . even in the political world. Except for the Rockefellers.

Now going back to the realism of the novel, which apparently some people have objected to, because it is too real, so real that they can't recognize it . . . yet you call the book a romance. At least this was on the original jacket.

It's still there.

Is this a defense against some criticism that you thought that you might get?

No. This was meant as a sort of typical Siouxland leg-pull. There are a lot of leg-pulls going on in the things I do. I mean them, but at the same time there is a little bit of a leg-pull. I won't say a joke, a practical joke. A Siouxlander has a priceless sense of humor. While you think he is being naïve, actually all along there is in him a piece of the Old Lizard back there which is quite aware of the humor of what he is doing in a given situation. Mark Twain has a lot of this in him. I meant that as a slight leg-pull. Women like to read romances and fantasies, you know, to comfort themselves. This is the way life should be, they think. When we know it is something else. So I thought, this is really a romance the way I've got it. This is the way a man looks at romance. To me, what I have in the book, that's romance for me.

In what respect? The excitement? Or the strangeness?

The truth. Great beauty in truth. There isn't much beauty in fantasy. Or in something that is prettified. But there is great beauty in truth. And I meant to make a real shaft of that word "romance." But I wanted to turn it around. And incidentally, the Old Ones, the guys far back that first used that term, they meant it somewhat that way. Hawthorne meant it a little bit that way. I forget . . . there is an Englishman that did too. Didn't Smollett say something about that too somewhere? And he writes very realistic novels.

> *Now, you mentioned all these things that were later, in a sense, proven true in Minneapolis. Is there anything in the novel which is completely invented? We mentioned the lady under the bridge. But now she, if she doesn't live there, she should.*

Yes.

> *There is the coal dock, and there are some shacks there, so this is easy to accept. And the University of Minnesota is there, and that's a school, more or less. What about the excursions into Siouxland, more or less?*

Well, of course I like to take a trip down here. When I used to live up there in Minneapolis I often drove down and I . . . oh, I wanted to contrast city and country, back and forth.

> *I have objected before, you know, that when you get over into South Dakota nothing happens. I forget where this occurs, but there is one seduction scene where the people walk through a state park or something for about ten pages.*

Oh, yes, almost thirty pages. That's near Pipestone. Pipestone National Monument.

> *You seem concerned at this point with the flowers, the weeds, the birds, the sounds, the countryside, and not a great deal happens.*

Well, there is a seduction at the end of that scene. One has to prepare for those. I like to walk around the countryside and see these things. I thought it'd be interesting for people to see how . . . the Siouxlander likes to walk through his own country and there are many of them who appreciate all of this. That's why I had Elizabeth, and Bert, I think it was, take this little tour. And I was kind of laughing a little at that kind of person, too (Elizabeth, that is), because I know the type. They are members of flower groups and so on, and they say this year we must get out to Gitchie Manitou Park, or this year we must go to the park down at Sioux City, and so on. I laugh a little bit at that; and at the same time I think that's fine. I wanted to have . . . but behind all that really . . . . I am starting to remember this book now. You see some of this stuff is so old now. My tendency is that once I've written a book I forget about it. I am busy with a new bunch of people. You know, living a whole new life. So it is hard for me to dredge this all up again. In fact, I have been a little amazed, almost dismayed, that I can remember it, which is probably not a good sign. I wanted . . . . It isn't just a single incident, as you will recall. That section is called "Siouxland Idyll" and I wanted to have an idyll in the "romance." How did they used to pronounce it in Chaucer's time? Something natural, rather beautiful, amongst all those rocks and stones, and finally this is what straightens Elizabeth out. She becomes a woman who can fall in love with this man whom she should have had in the beginning. Her problem with her brother, this brother–sister business, runs through the whole book. This idyllic little walk helped straighten her out. I am a great one for believing that nature does straighten people out. If you are in trouble, go out in the woods for a while.

This may be part of the problem of the metropolitan reader who finds it difficult to understand.

Yes.

That a walk in the woods or on the prairie can straighten out a character.

Yes. See the animals and see nature and see how things work.

Would these scenes be strong enough to make Morning Red *a Western novel? Now here we are dealing in categories which I know you like to avoid.*

Yes. Well, I think I would say that it is west of the Mississippi. It is a Midland novel in a sense. But I would say it is part of Western America. I am not sure that categories should be so narrow, say Western American letters, that you can't have these things in it.

No, it is a matter of Western flavor or attitude or something.

Yes, for example, I would call most of these Faulkner things Western America. It certainly isn't East. And I am not sure that I want to call it South even.

Let's get back to Monk for a minute and the Plato theory. The split . . .

That's where the word romance comes in too. That little subtitle really works. As you will notice, both boys, Kurt and Jack, have the usual problem of a young man trying to find that right woman, and they are looking around a little bit. Just as all men look for their soul mate. And so . . . Monk also has his problems. He too would like very much to find a soul mate. But for him the problem is out. So he is a perfect man to discuss Plato's theory.

And all three of them have trouble adjusting their male–female components, back and forth.

Yes. And that's why toward the end of the book, as I was writing it, I remembered that somewhere in my college days, my prof mentioned that Plato went into the business of soul mates. So I looked it up. I forget which book it was in where Plato describes how the original man was a four-legged creature, two-headed and four-legged.[3] Its faces faced outward and its legs faced outward. A hermaphrodite. These four-legged people pulled off some stunt that was wrong, and the gods became angry, and they took a knife and like you cut an apple in half, they cut them in half, the female side on one side and the male side on the other. These people soon had to begin searching to find each other, look

[3] *The Symposium.* FFM

for each other on earth, for their better half. Well, as man went on interbreeding and multiplying and becoming diversified upon the face of the earth, the problem of finding a true soul mate became more and more difficult. Your true soul mate may be on the other side of the earth and you may never have a chance to run into her. She may not be in your society at all. If Plato's theory is correct, it is a wonderful theory.

Yes, it is.

Also she may be of another age. Some people have said that I am a seventeenth-century man. Which makes me smile just a little bit. But suppose I am? How am I going to find my true mate in the twentieth century? Also, Plato brings out that some souls, that some halves, might not have been cut properly, that the female aspect may have fallen over onto the male side, and vice versa, so when they look for each other they may find that their true mate is in their own sex. But this was a wonderful theory, and I thought that this would help set up and explain a little bit why Kurt is having his problems in Jack.

Yes.

Of course this fits in with my idea of romance, why I used the word romance. This is really what I meant: these people are all busy searching for their true soul, their true mate, and as a result are finding the deeper reaches of happiness.

Well, this myth from Plato is very likely the background of the Christian notion of two becoming one in marriage.

Yes. That marriages are made in heaven.

Yes, and it is a matter of personalities being complemented.

That's right.

When a Western writer works in isolation, or so it seems, like you, Fisher, Stegner, Clark, Guthrie, Fergusson, Waters, all in a ring as it were, all around the Great Plains area, with none of you really within talking distance . . . this just bothers a person's work . . . when you do get a chance to talk with these men, as you did with Walter Clark and Fisher recently, does this add to your ideas, encourage you in your work? Or do you find yourself arguing with these people because you are so far apart? Do you get along with Clark, for example?

Oh, very well, very well. I didn't know what would happen in Clark's case. I met him last summer for the first time. On the way back from California, my wife and I drove back over the Sierras from Coarsegold and stopped at Virginia City in Nevada, the one that Mark Twain wrote about. We wanted to see some of that. I called his house in Reno from there. When he came to the phone I was surprised to find that he had a low and powerful voice, a resonant voice. I didn't know how he would take all this, but I said to him, "This is Frederick Manfred. If I threw my hat in the doorway, what would happen?" And he said, "Why don't you try it?" So I took him up on it and I said we would be over in about an hour or so. He gave me some directions that were kind of complicated. We drove up. His wife came out to visit us, to talk with us first — I thought maybe to sort of check us out. As I told my wife, "If it looks like we're not going to get along, we'll pull out. I don't want to be a pest to anyone." But it didn't take long and he stepped outdoors. He gradually warmed up. And after a little bit he got out some beer. Then a little later (you could tell we were getting along better and better) he suggested to his wife that she make lunch. So we wound up staying for a real nice long visit . . . oh, from around nine o'clock A.M. until around three o'clock P.M., I guess it was. We talked about the Old West.

We had a great time together. We saw eye to eye on many things. We talked about the corruption that creeps into little Western towns, that human nature seems to be the same the world over. The only difference is that it is Western corruption rather than, say, Eastern corruption. But we have our own. The effect of climate and terrain on people. How after a while the land seems to want to have its own way about what you do. I had a very good time with him. In fact, I don't think he and I had anything we differed on as much as I had later on with Vardis Fisher. I did lament a little bit when Clark told me that he had to spend so much time teaching. I said that I wished he had another ten books for us instead of just four. Well, he said that he had at least twenty-four plots very well worked out that he could have written all these years if he hadn't taught. I felt very sad about that. But he said he had resigned himself to the notion. He too felt sad about it. He thought if he could just get four more done, then he would be satisfied. Or at least he could say, "All right, I've at least done that much." He had resigned himself to only four more. Then at the end, as a kind of joke, I said . . . . Meanwhile, we hadn't asked each other about each other's work at all. I never discuss that. The same thing with all the good authors I have ever talked to. Somehow you just don't talk about your own book.

What about the publishing of them though?

Oh, yes, we do that. And common problems with publishers. How stupid some people are in the East, and so on. But never the contents and how we went about it. Never the techniques. Generally, possibly, but not particularly. . . . I said to him as we were about to leave — I'd picked up paperback copies of three of my books out of our car — I said, "You probably have some friends you've been wondering how you could get rid of with a present. You know you should give them something but you don't want to give them much. How about trying these out on them?" He laughed. And he said, "Well, you probably have three friends too that you need to take care of that way." So he went back into the house and got me three of his. So we exchanged books. That's the nearest we came to talking about them. Our talk tends to be . . . I won't say lofty, but downright. Down-to-earth and honest. Explosive. Takes off quite a lot . . . . Fisher we saw on that same trip. I had visited with him once before.[1] We drove from Reno where Clark lived up to the city of Hagerman, Idaho, where Fisher lived with his wife Opal. We were there three days. Had a great time. After about an hour or so . . . . That's the beauty of these people. The artists generally, when they recognize you as one of their own people, one of their clan, it's as if you have been with them all your life. They instantly plunge into intimate detail about truth, and the search for it, and at any given instance you can tell exactly how they think, what they think, how they feel about things. Which I love them for.

> *You think there is more of a common interest this way among the half-dozen Western writers than there is in the East?*

Oh, yes. My feeling is . . . the few times I have seen writers in the East together I've observed that there is an enormous amount of jealousy. Wrestling for position. They stick their face into the spotlight. Red Warren one time told me that the greatest competition he knew of was for first position by writers in the East. He said that the fight was deadly. I said to Red Warren one time, "You mean, say, between Robert Frost and Carl Sandberg?" And he said, "Oh, God, yes, especially Carl Sandberg." He said that the fight was saurian. Real lizards ready to gobble up the unwary stranger that comes around.[2] This surprised me. Because I have no sense of that in me. It's probably lurking in the background just a little bit, you know. No man wants to be wiped out. He wants to be heard. But certainly not in those few contacts that I have had with Western American writers have I seen anything of a jealous or envious nature. Everybody is delighted that it is going as well as it is. And that doesn't mean that we are patting each other on the back, either. Not at all. Fisher and I, for example, we argue on many subjects. He sees some things differently from me. Generally we look at life the same way. But on such things as whether the artist is more feminine

[1] Vardis and Opal Fisher came to visit us at Wrâlda in Bloomington, Minnesota. FFM

[2] This is my wording of his observation. FFM

than he is masculine, and the matter of whether the artist is a child and so on, I disagree with him. He has an abnormal admiration for womenfolks. Probably due to his admiration for his mother. He seems to think that the artistic instinct is strongly feminine. I . . . . Many other people do too, by the way. I see it the other way around. I think it is the stallion in us that is the artist. Now if you look at nature in the animal kingdom, for example, particularly, say, in horses, and you go to any little farm where they raise ponies — ponies still happen to be quite wild in some respects . . . . Better, if you study a wild stallion, which I did by glasses when I was up in the Big Horns one time. I found a wild white stallion up west of the Big Horn. They'd never been able to catch him, either by airplane (I guess they could by helicopter) and they had never been able to catch him on horseback. Watching him . . . . You have one male running the band, the mares and the little ones. He has to be the sharpest and most sensitive to his environment at all times for his band to survive. He tends to be extremely sensitive, the male, the head male. Whereas the female is sharply sensitive about the time she is about to have her colt. He is also the most inventive. He responds to sunlight, fresh smells of winds, and knows where to find the best place to eat, the best and sweetest clovers, and the best grasses, et cetera. This is true even in the chicken kingdom. It's always the rooster who calls over the hens to tell them, here's a pretty stone or a big kernel. "Come over here. Cuk-cuk-cuk." You know. "This is lovely. Come on, girls." So to me, I feel that it's the sensitive stallion in us that is basically the creator. In our world, the human world, he is the man who builds. He projects towers, builds bridges, symphonies, skyscrapers. Womenfolk don't have much instinct for that. I think they have an instinct that tends to protect and hold. Compassionate at the same time that they possess. They are holders. Well, he, Fisher, and I disagree on that, of course.

> *I wonder if woman is a better researcher.*
>
> Yes, I think she could well be.
>
> *Fisher has done many historical novels and has done detailed research. Would this perhaps par-*

tially support the feeling he has for women as artists?

Could be.

Getting it confused with woman as researcher.

Just exactly backwards, to me anyway. A great attention to details. He also made the remark that most artists are fools and children when it comes to business matters. Well, that makes me smile. Because I always thought that people who worried about how much money they were going to get for doing something, for dickering, that when you went into a store and began arguing over how much you were going to pay, haggle over prices, that that was childish. To me. I think you are really mature when you don't worry about a price. You assume that the other guy is as mature as you are, that he will give you the exact right price. That's the maturity we are going towards. If we have to aim ourselves the other way, being worried continually that the other guy is going to rupe us, why then we are going downhill. We are unraveling as a civilization rather than building up. . . . I wonder, could I comment a little about my experiences at the Huntington Hartford Foundation? I was there last year. Up until that time I had always been a little apologetic about being called an artist. You know, they're supposed to be a little odd, crackpots, et cetera. They're flighty and irresponsible. Jumpy. Can't depend upon them. All that. Well, here we have sixteen cabins there, or sixteen studios. They (the fellows, the artists) came from four fields, sculpturing, painting, writing, and music. All four originals.

Were they from all parts of the country?

All over the world, too. There were some from Afghanistan, India, Japan, Hungary, France, England, Germany. My stay happened to overlap a period when there was a change of groups coming in. I was terribly impressed by such things as this. Here is Huntington Hartford, who owns this place, who is worth I don't know how many million, fifty, sixty, maybe more than that, who probably uses the Foundation as sort of a tax write-off — I don't know what his arrangements are — at any rate, he could certainly afford to pay for any overdue postage. Well, here was one of these artists who had a modest income. Not much as a painter. There is an overdue stamp due and the notice comes in her mailbox that "You owe the Foundation five cents." She didn't bother to wait until the next day to pay it; she ran right back right then and got the five cents. Brought it right over. Painstaking. They tend to all be that. I was terribly proud of them. This was the kind of people I was told when I was a young man that ministers were supposed to be like. Missionaries, perhaps. Well, I didn't find ministers to be like that in my lifetime; certainly not all of them. Some of them I have. I've run into some very fine ministers in the last few years. But these people, these artists, were to me the real children of God. This is . . . . The highest a man can become is to be one of these artists. It's true that they look a little foolish to other people, because they happen to be so plain-spoken, and because they take strong positions. But this is because they somehow manage to keep a child's innocence while looking for truth, seeing what it is, developing it, and making this natural bent find adult truth. I was delighted with them.

> *We sometimes confuse irresponsibility with innocence, maybe.*

Yes we do. I think there is a great deal of jealousy of them on the part of other people in other occupations. You know, it's difficult to accept someone who is better than you.

> *Oh, yes.*

And especially in a democracy. In Europe, you know, they're used to having an aristocracy. In Europe they have a far different attitude toward their writers. In their minds. They honor them and worship them. Almost too much. Here we have an overly healthy cynicism, a skepticism, about our creative people. We tend to want to cut them down. We have gone a little too far the other way.

> *Now in spite of these various differences with Fisher when you visited him, isn't it true that he has to be called the Dean of Western novelists?*
> Oh, yes.

Not only because of the bulk of the work, but because of the talent involved there?

He has done more than some of us. Oh, yes.

Far more than most. I think you come second now in number of books.

It doesn't make any difference to me. He is a great man. When you are around him for a while you know that you are in the presence of a very great man. I have met quite a few writers. I have met Red Lewis — I knew him quite well.[3] And Robert Penn Warren. And John Dos Passos — spent a week with him one time. And I've met Allen Tate, Jimmy Farrell, Saul Bellow, and some of the others. But none of them come up to Fisher as far as . . . not only in their work but as a man personally . . . . Hemingway committed suicide. Vardis, by the way, often talks about that. He wants to do it too, he says. But there is always the sense that the Old Lizard in him is standing apart and smiling over this. I don't think his Old Lizard will ever let him.

He used to joke about waiting until he could take the book editor of Time *magazine with him.*

Well, he's changed that story now. Yes. He is now a little angry at the funeral directors. That you can't get permission to bury yourself on your own land, et cetera, that you have to be buried in an approved cemetery.

What was the story they told about loading himself with dynamite?

He had it all figured out. You see, if you disappear, drown, then you just disappear, and you aren't officially dead.[4] They still win out. But he wanted to be sure that this (his suicide and disappearance on his own land) would be officially recorded. He was going to invite the local county attorney and . . . what's the guy that's a doctor? — the one they call to see if you're

---

[3] [Sinclair Lewis.]

[4] The wife cannot inherit the property until the husband has been officially declared dead. FFM

dead or not . . . the coroner, and the sheriff, and take a little walk with them. He wouldn't tell them he'd loaded himself up with dynamite and a fuse. He'd take them to an open place on this twenty acres he had there, and then after a bit he'd say, "Say, would you guys mind standing here a minute? I should go over there and check out that line fence." Then when he's about fifty or sixty feet away and has made sure they're looking at him, he's going to touch himself off. He says, "All they'll find is a belt buckle and fingernails." He says, "Then they have got to record me as being officially dead and buried on my own property." [Laughter.] I thought that was a great story. I told him that if he went out that way it wouldn't be as sad an ending as Hemingway's. It would be a glorious ending. He'd go out in a brilliant flash of light, rather than as Hemingway did with a shotgun blast alone by himself. Well, Vardis is wonderful that way. We had a just simply marvelous time. From about four o'clock in the afternoon that first day on, it was just sort of a dream world. By this time we were thoroughly awake, following everything around. Music and . . . it's almost impossible to report it. Around ten, eleven o'clock, you know, we'd have our dinner. That late. We'd be too busy talking. It was wonderful, you know. There was no sense of time. It just seemed to go on and on. Then when we were about to leave, Vardis was kind of cool, sort of standoffish. His eyes glittered. Tears kind of came into his eyes once. But you knew how he was feeling. Then I was quite startled. As we left the door he did something that we men do in our family. He suddenly threw his arms around me and gave me a great big kiss, and then turned around and walked off. That was the end of the visit. You know. No good-byes. Just walked away.

> *He has often suggested in his work a very curious problem in Western literature. Vardis is always pleading for a rational approach. And this is partly why he goes through the scholarly business of accumulating all this work, of getting his ideas. And yet he argues that point so hard that he becomes irrational while doing it.*

That's because he is an artist. He knows that after you are through with research it is still the irrational, it is still the intuitive, the instinctive part of man that is the real artist.

You wouldn't call this Western then? You think the same thing happens in the East? That a certain kind of irrationality follows the preliminaries?

Yes, I think so.

Because of the closeness to nature out here and because nature has these extremes, hot and cold temperatures, the high mountains, the low plains, et cetera, people tend to accuse Western literature of being too irrational.

You can't be. We are continually being stretched so far back and forth. For example, when Shakespeare in that scene of his in *King Lear* with thunder and lightning going on . . . it's terribly dramatic in Shakespeare. He probably never saw more than a half-dozen thunderstorms in Great Britain. They only have a sort of muddled, a mumbled kind of thunderstorm in Great Britain. While we really have them out here. The British have never seen a tornado. They never have one. Not even a waterspout. We have tornadoes. Oh . . . how many . . . ten, twenty a year out here on the plains? We know a lot about them. So for us to get nature in as Shakespeare loaded it into his work . . . well, we still haven't developed the language and the technique to get it in. We'll have to work out of the irrational side of ourselves even more than we do. We'll have to open up the scope, let out our antennae, stretch our personality and ego, to get it in. We are just beginning our great civilization here. We are just starting.

Which writers do you think are coming closer, excluding yourself?

Well, I'd say Frank Waters and Clark and Fisher. To me they are about the three best writers we've produced in America. I'd rate them ahead of Hemingway. Faulkner? I don't quite know what to say there. Old Bill was quite a fellow. Full of the old dinosaurs. There are a lot of dinosaurs crawling around in

his things. But I haven't made up my mind yet where I want to place that fellow. He may just sink away because of his many obscurities.

That's possible.

And that he wasn't always clear. But he had his eye on the ball, though. He really knew what was going on.

What about Guthrie and Stegner? Those two are a little bit on the periphery of this whole business.

I would agree that they are on the periphery. Stegner hasn't really made up his mind whether he is West or East. He makes too many apologies for what he is. He shouldn't do that. You don't have to apologize for what you are out here. Some people call us the rednecks and the roughnecks. That to me is a great tribute. I would rather be a Western American roughneck than I would be a suave caballero in Spain, or a suave cavalier in France, or a suave gentleman in England. To be a maverick out here is as good as anything. We are just beginning our civilization. Our Shakespeares are still ahead. I hope we aren't destroyed so they get a chance to do it.

Now we are using a rather rough word, maverick, to describe people. You have often talked in terms of a rose, a delicate flower, as part of your own theory of writing. How does this jell?

Well, a little while ago we were talking about music, how Thurs aspired to get up to that very highest reach. I have an Aunt Kathryn who complains rather bitterly about some of my rough realistic scenes. And I have had some ministers and even some members of my family go after me. After thinking about this for quite a while, I finally came up with the following theory. I've sometimes asked them, "What do you think is beautiful?" "Well, a flower." "What flower?" "Well, a rose." It occurred to me one day that a rose petal by itself isn't very beautiful. Or even a flower by itself. How did it get there? To me what is beautiful is the entire rose. The whole rose. First you have just earth. The earth lay inert for a long time. Gradually it began to stir and out of it things began to grow. So you have first the earth, the humus, even manure, dirt, fungus, crawling bugs, bacteria. Out of this a stem rises, a stalk. Leaves form on it. Then finally at the top you have the petal. Beauty is the whole rose *in situ*. In the natural situation. That's beauty. That's everything. So the writer tries to get everything into his books. He describes the earth and the dirt, he describes the stems and leaves, he mentions the thorn, and then he finally gets around to the petal. It's all in his work. Now some authors dwell too much on the petal. Now, how long does a rose petal last between the leaves of, say, the Bible even? In a week it's dried up and gone. Doesn't mean anything. It lasts, though, for a little time if it stands out there in nature, in full life. Some authors spend most of their time on the manure or the dirt side. Farrell. Possibly Miller. Et cetera. Well, to me that isn't quite right either. Every man has his own notion of how much of each part he should get in. But to me . . . maybe I should backtrack here. I once had an editor who believed that only certain things had a place in literature. Only certain things have their place in books. I told him he had that all wrong. I said that literature was a world-and-life view, that everything had its place in literature.

> *A writer goes everywhere and is obligated to deal with all of it.*

Deal with all of it and put it in. He is sort of an overall composer. A maker.

> *Which is a curious thing. Western literature, which is accused of being regional, is actually much less regional than most Eastern literature being produced today.*

There is a chance that we are producing universal things in our Western kind of making.

> *And apparently what we have to do is shake off the stereotype cowboy story, the various myths that have been exploited on television.*

And be careful of critics from other countries coming in. Because, like the Frenchmen, they say, "Oh, the cowboy! the cowboy!" I think they're hitting on something that's true. But we had better take a good look at what they are saying. They may be picking out a fad, a fad aspect in us, and I wouldn't want that.

No.

Then there are those who say that the best part of us is the Indian. Well, again we must watch that. Oliver La Farge overstrokes that a little bit.

Particularly in Laughing Boy.

Yes.

The defense in the picture books or the history books is another thing.

D. H. Lawrence raises some great points in his *Studies in Classic American Literature*. But again, he comes in as an outsider, almost as an intruder. He tries to tell us what we should be doing, what we should be thinking, and how we should regard our Indian. And if you study his books about America, aren't they sort of strained? What is it, like in his . . .

The Plumed Serpent.

. . . written a little on the strained side? The difference between Frank Waters and D. H. Lawrence is the difference between the master and the intruder. Waters knows what he is doing . . . . Anything I'd tell Waters to do, I suppose he'd have something to tell me to do in return. That would be fair. But he could have spent just a little more time on storytelling.[5] To me the greatest of all arts, finally and at long last (I have tried a lot of different things in my own life, and in my own writing) the greatest thing of all things is to become a good storyteller. If you tell a good story, you have a chance to get a good many different kinds of responses from different people. Many people will read it. And if you are a very good storyteller, you can also tell it in such a manner that the profound will like it. So to write a story that is not just a story, but a profound one, that's the greatest of all.

[5] I've since met Frank Waters many times. He too has all the movements of a great man. FFM

In 'forty-nine, 'fifty, and 'fifty-one you published three novels as a trilogy, The Primitive, The Brother, *and* The Giant, *which have during the past year . . . or is it a year and a half now? . . . have been reissued by Alan Swallow in Denver with the new title* Wanderlust, *with some rewriting. Well, from 'forty-nine to 'sixty-three, some fourteen years, what made you go back to that? Redo it?*

Well, there were a number of things. The idea for it occurred even during the time I was doing the last novel [*The Giant*]. You see, I was somewhat caught a little like Dickens was caught in his day. He wrote for magazines, a chapter each week or whatever it was, and once it was in print he was caught by what was in print and he couldn't go back and change something. If a character wanted to go off on a new track or if he [Dickens] decided he had the wrong name for something, he couldn't go back and change it. I was somewhat the same way. Doubleday was my publisher at the time. They'd heard that I was working on a big book. Doubleday has a tendency to hurry the author along. They want a lot of books. They have what I call the scatter-gun method of publishing.

The big list.

Yes, and they hope that if they can publish two or three hundred books in a year that two or three will become best sellers. Then they concentrate on those three. So they are always urging their authors to hurry up and get something ready. Also, I was a little close with money at the time. So when they asked me what this book was about, I said it really probably was a trilogy. It was divided naturally into three subjects and was going to be quite long. Run over a thousand pages. They suggested that I could publish it in sections. Then when it was all done, they'd put it in one volume, as was done in the case of *USA* by John Dos Passos and *Studs Lonigan* by Jimmy Farrell. I said all right. But you see what happens. You get the first book in print while you're working on the second one, and at that time you suddenly discover that you made an error in the first part. Not really an error, but you want to do something in the second one and you have to go back and change something in the first. Clean it up a little bit. Rearrange it. Or cut it even. Well, I was caught by that and I got swung around by what was going on in the first volume. In the third volume, the same thing. So almost from the beginning I knew that someday I would probably have to do something more with that work. It's a mistake to let a publisher have a piece of something before you are done with it. If you come to an editor with a half-done book, he is loaded with ideas on how you should do it. He is a little less apt to tell you how to do it after it is finished. He picks up the finished thing and it looks like it is final. But you show somebody something that is half done and right away you have a thousand advisors. This was the same way with that work. I got a lot of advice on that when it was still unfinished. The reviewers of the first book would say, well, I hope he does so and so with the next book. You see, these reviewers . . . . You shouldn't do that. The whole book should be done in total isolation so it has a chance to come out with the author's total stamp on all of it. About nineteen fifty-five or 'fifty-six, when I was doing *Morning Red*, I just for the fun of it . . . not just for the fun of it, really, but for an exercise . . . had to see in a trial run just how many words I could knock out of the trilogy. A few people had said that I'd become a little wordy. Some were saying that I really was drifting out to become the Tom Wolfe kind of writer. So I went over twenty or thirty pages, and I discovered that just knocking out a word here and there that wasn't doing the job. I could cut it considerably if I was really going to rewrite it. Somewhere around 'fifty-seven, I think, I began reworking it in earnest. In the pages of the published book I would clean up, say, four or five pages, cut it all up, and then type it up in a new draft. Then I saw that even that wasn't thoroughgoing enough. So I backed up once more and I practically rewrote the whole work again, you might say, from scratch. With the other one (the published book) in front of me, I condensed it. I changed names in it. I cut it from 1280 pages,

I think it was, to 727 pages. And I have more in it now than I had in it the other way. It's compressed. The story runs more lean. I took out some of these little experimental paragraphs, et cetera. They were kind of abstract passages, exercises, just as abstract art is really kind of an exercise. It really isn't art itself, but is an exercise in art. I wanted to have a good story that many people could read, and that for the few discerning readers, the ones that I really want to appeal to and draw, they would find a really profound story at work. I wanted to make the style harder. By this time I had also written *Lord Grizzly*, where I learned something about style that I hadn't learned before. By then I'd started *Riders of Judgment* and got some of that Western twang going in my head, the hardness of it . . . I'd met a number of those cowboys who said "Not yit!" . . . that was all at work in my head when I was rewriting this. Every year I would do about a hundred pages, maybe two hundred pages, and I finally had it all typed up. The curious thing was that in New York, they weren't interested in publishing this any more. Doubleday, et cetera. Meanwhile Swallow had been urging me . . . . There was one man in New York who was interested in this. A man named Herb Alexander of Pocket Books.

> *Isn't it part of the problem there that they have to overcome the critical opinion of the first edition?*

Yes.

> *And they aren't willing to do that always?*

Funny thing is that it was just the New York critics who were rough on that one. I had had very fine . . .

> *Yes,* Time *magazine.*

Time magazine gave me the business, so to speak.* And in the *New York Times Book Review* . . . . They all meet in their little cocktail parties, and they all know each other, and they all run back and forth like schools of sharks. First they eat up the

---

* On only the first volume of the trilogy, *The Primitive*. They ignored volumes two and three, *The Brother* and *The Giant*. FFM

people on one end of the ocean and then they come and eat up the people on the other end. You never quite know where that school of sharks is heading next.

> *Part of the criticism you got from friends at the time, I think, was valid, that of too much youthful exuberance.*

Oh yes.

> *But this wasn't what the Eastern critics picked up.*

Oh no. They were going after something else.

> *They made fun of it.*

But they were wrong. Whereas some of my few friends, and some of the Western fellows who reviewed it, also made the remark that it had too much youthful exuberance. And Swallow. Swallow said, "What you have done here, Fred, is you've sent your first draft out." Which was true. Also I think I was a little overconcerned there. . . . In the construction of that work I had the problem of knowing too much before I began. In *This Is the Year* I think I had only about twenty-eight or thirty pages of a sort of rough outline or a jotting down of the sequence of events with the detail that I wanted to get into each section. But with the trilogy *Wanderlust*, for its original version I had over a hundred and twenty, maybe a hundred thirty, pages of real fine note-taking for the plot. Where everything went. This is to lead to that, and this is to follow that, and this means this, and this movement here is eventually going to end up being reactivated over here. I was quite profoundly struck by music, how a symphony is built. I took a course in that from Madame Stokowski, on music appreciation, and she analyzed Beethoven's First Symphony, how it has three movements in it, and how themes are introduced and then the counterpoint, et cetera, in sonata form. I tried to work that scheme all the way through that book. . . . It is curious, really, how *Morning Red* is really in some ways a piece of music too. It is loaded with counterpoint. Not one motion happens on, say, the Kurt side but what something like it occurs over on the Jack side. And it all came about somewhat naturally. Almost as if you were a Solomon.

Or a mother of a family. One boy voices his opinion and so you had to let the other boy voice his opinion in turn. In sort of a natural sequence. Well, in *Wanderlust*, that went a little differently, as far as counterpoint goes. There I was interested mostly in having the same theme come through in three different ways, in three different sections of the book. I had become interested in . . . we were talking a little bit ago about these split-apple people, the sorb apple, the gods cutting these four-legged people in half. I was also interested at that time [while doing *Wanderlust*] in eternal forms. Remember how Thurs went into this business about there being a thousand basic human forms and how they keep working through all life and repeating themselves? Well this, of course, is a musical concept. And since Thurs is a musician . . . . Have you ever wondered why I wrote about a musician instead of a writer?

> *Well, on the surface it seems obvious that if you were Thurs to a certain extent, and you were a writer, you simply wanted to disguise it a little.*

Well, maybe I wanted to disguise it too. I don't remember if I had that in mind at the time or not. Probably so. But the real reason was that I had become enamored of music and discovered to my astonishment that I had more music in me than I knew. My voice changed when I was very young . . . I guess I was something like ten or eleven years old. Ten years old my voice changed about a week before the Christmas program. Up to that time I was a good singer in the grade school and in the grammar school. I always sang in church programs. But suddenly my voice changed. The teacher who was teaching music at the time noticed something was wrong. He had everybody in the chorus take turns not singing — until they found me. Then they knew that I was the guy that was throwing them off. It was too late to kick me out of the group (for pride's sake), so he said, "Why don't you just move your mouth and pretend you're singing?" I was overly self-conscious after that about my singing. I also knew that when I was off, I really was off. This should have told me something. Or some music teacher should have said, "Well, Fred, if you know you're so bad you must have a keen ear." I didn't learn about the keen ear until I was thirty-five years old . . . . When I took this course from Madame Stokowski (in the summer of nineteen forty-seven), I also thought I would take up some form of actually playing something and I decided that I would play the piano. I had big hands. The music teacher told me, after about ten minutes of trying me out, that I had perfect pitch, something I never knew. This accounts in part for the fact that I couldn't sing. My voice probably was not too good to begin with, but this ear said "Hey, you're way off. You better shut up." I was always self-conscious about it. I couldn't get my voice connected with what my ear told me it should be. Never could get the two together. I always knew when it was off. Another reason why the work had a musician for a hero was I had been moved sometimes more by a phrase in music than by a phrase in writing. I have had it already while listening to symphonies, or at home lying on the floor while listening to a good record, or hearing my mother sing a little (marvelous voice, a country church voice), and other people, that it suddenly would be as though my whole nervous system would be on fire. I remember one occasion. I was attending a symphony in Minneapolis, the Minneapolis Symphony Orchestra. They were playing a piece by Tchaikovsky that gradually took hold . . . . No, it wasn't quite that way. Something in me suddenly awoke and wanted to get out of me. And I literally had tremors of fire running up and down my backbone. I thought I was going to go wild. I had an impulse to jump up and start skipping along over the tops of the seats. I wanted to jump up in the gallery. I really thought I was going out of my mind there for a little. Not in an insane sense, but in a sense of sheer ecstasy, one of the highest exultations any human being can get into. My whole nervous system was on fire. Great. Glorious. At that moment you couldn't have told me that I was a mortal, that I had bathroom duties, say, once a day. I couldn't have got that into my head at such a moment. This is the kind of thing that Shelley at his highest moments strives for. And of course falls down. While the cynics sit back and cut you all up. The creators make these wild explosions into the empyrean blue. That's why I wanted to have Thurs go into music. Because I thought I could write something that would really be moving. Because I was moved occasionally by a piece of music. . . . I think too that it is possible, perhaps, that I may have been . . . had I started early enough . . . had some teacher caught me very early with this so-called perfect pitch, and the fact that I've always had tunes running through my head, and the fact that when I would hear a horse clopping down the street the next thing you know, in the old days at least, my mind would start inventing on the sounds, playing around with them — a teacher would have told me that I was probably a composer, really.

Do you think really that this is the ultimate vision for Thurs then? You know he — in three volumes in the original edition — he tries Christianity of a certain kind with Calvin College first, and isn't satisfied with that, then he gets involved in Marxism in New Jersey, and finally in Minneapolis he becomes acquainted with Bruce Farrewell, the scientist, and science fails him.

Yes.

In fact it kills him in the first edition. Well, now, overriding all of this, then would you say that music or art is the ultimate vision for Thurs?

Yes. I would say so.

These other things are all minor problems.

Yes, they are. In my scheme of the hierarchy of the valuable that the human being gets involved in, the creative arts are tops.

Above all of these?

I used to think that music was the highest of all the arts. Now, probably because I am stuck with writing, I now think that writing a novel or drama is the highest of all arts. It involves more knowledge, a greater range of information. A greater range of talents is necessary to become a good writer.

This is why many novelists are beginning to claim that the novel is a better, a more complex, a more enduring form than poetry.

Yes.

Which I would argue with at the moment. But there is something to it.

Well, if poetry took the form of, say, the old epics, then I would argue too.

With a story line.

That's right. Then I would argue too. Because you see, what you are doing there, you are getting music up into the feel of . . . the timbre of music up into the word. But a great novelist should be able to . . . . You see, we have Tolstoy and Drieser and Dickens with a kind of a crude fumbling style. They are not really what you would call masters of style. Not at all. But they've got the stuff, though. They are impressive and tremendous, gigantic, for the material they have in there and the general narration. But they still really are not stylists. Now the last generation or two in American letters, and in English too, we are developing pretty fine stylists. The guys write very well today.

And say very little.

We still haven't put together the two, the real stuff.

In your earlier work, it seemed to me for a while it was possible to do this in two books, that is, Grizzly *as the example of craftsmanship and then the trilogy as a vision. Now the question will be whether* Wanderlust, *the revised version, does actually achieve some kind of union of the two.*

It may a little bit. But I hope to write a whole lot better book. I have some ideas for the future and if I just live long enough, keep my youth, I think I can do it. *Wanderlust* is about the best I can do at the moment over a wide scope. It is quite a complex book in its own right. It is . . . it was meant to be a symphony in words and a study of a man searching for ultimate happiness. Looking for it first in Christianity and so-called moral problems, and then, say, in economic problems, and then in the world of things, science, and not ever finding it, and finally going back to childlike worship, the search for beauty . . . no, not the search for beauty, but the expression of a beauty that he finds within himself. I think the remarkable thing about it is that he finds it within himself.

> *I think the remarkable thing about it is that while it is clearly an American book, it also contains within it the broad social concern of, say, the nineteenth-century British novel.*

There is more going on in that book than meets the eye. Getting back to what we said earlier about the pheasant that flies, works, you know . . . I was pretty conscious when I was doing that thing, this big complicated outline all worked out, and all these movements which I allowed for, along with, say, easy adjustment (if something wanted to go a little differently I let it go) . . . . But there are many strands going on and they all pretty well work. They do what I wanted them to do. It isn't just a simple autobiography. Oh no. It's a complicated book. More than most people think. If they will just dig around a little bit, they . . . . You see, in some ways my books are a little like myself. I don't often look at mirrors, or portraits of myself, but I have a sort of a notion of how I must feel to other people. When they first meet me, they think, here is a kind of a great big genial lummox. You know. And he has these big hands, and they are a little like a farm boy's hands in some ways, though no longer with calluses on them, except on the fingertips where they touch the pen and the typewriter. Then, as they become acquainted with him, they discover . . . well, they forget a little bit about my big hands and feet and they begin to see that maybe I've read a little bit. I really have only one or two good friends with whom I have ever opened up myself, have been confidential and close. They tell me, when we are being real frank with each other, that they wish that we could live together for another fifty years so they would get to know me better. What they have found so far they like very much. But they keep finding new layers to go down into. This is something I can't help. I was raised to be natural and friendly and warm and confidential and I am that to a point. But. And my books are like this too. On the surface they are congenial and sort of like a big lummox. But.

Speaking of friends learning to know you over a period of time, how has Calvin College received you since the publication of The Primitive?

Calvin wasn't very friendly to me after I graduated. But I was kind of a problem child there, I guess. I didn't do any harm to anyone. I didn't wreck any buildings or anything. But I was a problem child in ideas with them. How could such a nice fellow be so wrong? That was their attitude, you see. I remember that the first few times I drifted back onto the campus I received a pretty frosty reception from the profs. Then when the first version of the trilogy came out, book by book . . . . They didn't bother to read the whole work. They just read *The Primitive* and stopped dead there. Which they thought was supposed to be about Calvin. Actually . . . I put a lot of things in there that never happened at Calvin at all, things that came from other denominational schools, where my family, members of my family, and friends around here went. They didn't realize either that Thurs gets his just deserts at the end, in the third volume. They thought, you know, that I was trying to show that they were dead wrong and that Thurs was dead right and that was all. In some ways he was wrong too. So, had they read the whole work, they would have felt better about it. As the years went by, though, the younger generation coming in read it and they bent the profs a little bit. After all, profs do change a little bit if the pressure gets strong enough. I was astounded with . . . . When we had a class reunion in nineteen fifty-nine, I went back for it. I made up my mind I was just going to go in and see the fellows that were in my class and get out. I thought, you know, that the rest of them wouldn't want to see me. But to my great astonishment, I was . . . . I walked across the campus, and within ten minutes, the new development secretary, who was promoting a bigger Calvin, as they call it, a greater Calvin, put me up in what they call the Gold Room of the big house or the mansion they now own. The next thing, I was asked to meet some kids in the English Club, some ten or fifteen kids in a cozy corner somewhere. I showed up for this about five minutes early the next morning. To my astonishment the whole Commons was jammed. They had all decided to come and see me, see what I was going to say. I thought at the time, you know, that this was what they were thinking: "Come and see this monster, this horrible Benedict, hater of Christian faith," et cetera. Someone introduced me to the crowd. It was obvious they couldn't all hear me, so a prof called out very loudly, "Why don't we go over to the college auditorium, the chapel?" It was agreed to. Some kids flew out of the Commons building and sailed up to the main college building and opened every classroom door they could and hollered in, "That Feikema Manfred guy is going to talk down in chapel!" The kids would get up out of class without waiting for the prof to dismiss them and ran down there. Someone sailed through the seminary and it went the same way. Doors were opened, profs were caught short in the middle of a sentence, you know, and deserted. All went down there. Then the profs followed. By the time we had the thing set up to talk, somebody quickly put on a tape. So all this went down on the tape. The place was jammed. The aisles were full. All the fire ordinances were violated. They were sitting up on the platform with me. I spent two hours answering questions. This went on and on, from about ten-twenty A.M. until twelve-thirty P.M. It was warm and it was good. There were some really shotgun questions asked. I remember that I invented a theory right there on the platform. Some kid asked me something about where do we writers get our ideas. There was another writer present. I had invited Meindert De Jong to meet the English Club kids with me. He sat with me. At one time he spoke during the session. He agreed with me that it is as if another hand is helping us write, like it did the old Bible masters. That there is another spirit that tells us what to do. You might call it the Dinosaur. Or the Old Goat. Or the Old Adam. Then some kid said, "Well, how do you know but what this voice you hear isn't the voice of the devil instead of the voice of God?" It was a tough question to answer in that spot. But I went after it. I said each man had to answer that for himself. But it was my feeling that if we accept the existence of God, that we'd have to say God was a complicated fellow, that he wasn't just a . . . that the path to God was perhaps an exceedingly narrow one, all right, but that there were probably a number of narrow paths up there. Not only was there one that the theologians had worked out, but there was possibly an artistic path up there too. That if you could be saved by theology, you could also be saved by art. That in the final analysis I thought that perhaps God was a very great artist, a greater artist than he was a theologian . . . . You know, that went over very well with them. They took that in stride. Because in a sense that is good Calvinistic doctrine. The individual approach to God. That the way is narrow, et cetera. The moment the program was over the theologians wanted me to come over to the seminary and defend my theory, or at least expound my theory. They thought that I had worked this out very carefully earlier. Actually, I made it up as I was standing there. That was a great day. I was so excited I couldn't sleep for about two days afterwards. You know. The Old Mother, so to speak, had allowed me to come back and had treated me warmly. I have been invited every year since then to come back. Was invited again this year . . .

The text of *Conversations with Frederick Manfred* was set in Intertype Baskerville with the aid of ligatures, logotypes, and specially engraved matrices. The display type is handset Baskerville Foundry.

Typography by Donald M. Henriksen.

Cover: *Strathmore* Grandee Duplex, Basque Brown/Cordoba Brown; text paper: *Warren* Olde Style Wove; printed by the University of Utah Printing Service; bound by Mountain States Bindery.